I also dedicate my book to my children

Kylie and Guy

I made a promise to myself as I grew up that I show love and support to my children when I had them. I have tried very hard to keep my promise. I know I have slipped up more than once with my forgiving children.

No child deserves to be ill-treated, especially my own. I have hopefully corrected my mistakes made with my kids, showing a much softer, playful and loving side to my grandchildren. My newfound unconditional love is now shared with each new generation.

For Kylie and Guy:

I am sorry my hurts and insecurities became
your roadmap as you grew up.
I am sorry I wasn't stronger than my self-doubt and unpredictability.
I am sorry you weren't always protected from my mental health issues.
Always remember my love for you both will never waver.
Always remember you are both my greatest achievements.
Always remember being your proud mum is an honour.
Watching you both grow into caring, loving
and strong adults is my blessing.
Thank you for believing in me.

When the Mind Divides

Lost Innocence. Lost Time. Lost Self.

JO WILCOX

When the mind divides: Lost Innocence. Lost Time. Lost Self.

Reader advice: This book contains personal accounts of traumatic abuse, including emotional, physical and sexual violence. Some scenes may be distressing or activating for survivors. Please take care while reading and pause if you need to. Support resources are listed at the back of this book for anyone who may feel impacted.

This memoir is a recounting of personal experiences and memories as perceived and remembered by the author.

While every effort has been made to present an authentic portrayal of events, emotions and relationships, it is important to note that memory is fallible and subjective.

Names, dates and details have been included to the best of the author's recollection and understanding at the time of writing. Some details have been changed to protect the privacy of some individuals. Dialogues and interactions are based on the author's recollection and may not be verbatim.

Front cover image Shutterstock

Published by Jo Wilcox with support from Ignite & Write Publishing
www.igniteandwritepublishing.com

IGNITE & WRITE

ISBN: 978-1-7645952-0-9 (pbk) 978-1-7645952-1-6 (ebook)

NATIONAL LIBRARY OF AUSTRALIA

A catalogue record for this book is available from the National Library of Australia

Dedicated to my amazing grandson, Oscar.

Always in my heart.

Never forgotten.

Contents

Foreword

It is impossible to read this book without thinking: *how much suffering can one person endure in their lifetime?* But that is only part of this story. It is equally impossible to not be moved by the resilience of the human spirit, the courage it takes to heal, the persistent effort required to break intergenerational cycles, and the restorative power of love.

Yes, this story is about resilience, and a testament to what someone can endure and overcome. But the heart of this story is about family – about the potential for trauma within a family to destroy a soul, and the potential for love of family to restore it. Throughout this raw and heartfelt memoir, Jo reflects on how her love and commitment to her family, particularly her children and grandchildren, have been both a source and motivator for healing and, in some cases, for her very survival.

In my many years of work supporting victim-survivors of child sexual abuse, I have come to understand what it takes for someone to disclose the abuse they have experienced. Sexual abuse thrives on secrecy. Perpetrators of child sexual abuse know the tactics needed to guarantee this silence, and to simultaneously shift ownership of shame from themselves to the innocent children they choose to abuse. As Jo so clearly demonstrates in this memoir, the effects of child sexual abuse and the associated internalised shame can be debilitating and enduring.

Jo's courage to first disclose the abuse she experienced to her doctor, and then to other professionals, and ultimately culminating with this book, can therefore not be underestimated. Breaking the silence was something Jo was taught to fear from a very young age. And yet, Jo no longer wants to hold this fear. Rather, she wants her story to help other survivors consider if they can also let go of theirs. Jo acknowledges how long these tactics of fear, shame and secrecy left her feeling alone in her efforts to cope, understand and heal.

You will learn through this book that in spite of the lack of compassion shown to Jo by too many people throughout her life, she has not lost her ability to offer love and compassion to others. By her own admission, offering this to herself is still a work in progress. Jo is offering this memoir, despite the fear and anxiety it triggers, in the hope that other victim-survivors will feel less alone in their own experience of recovery, know that help is available and understand it is never too late to reach out for it.

In this book, Jo has shared the personal and professional support she has found helpful. This support has included specialised sexual assault counselling, a therapeutic intervention for trauma known as EMDR, understanding her diagnosis of Dissociative Identity Disorder, the power of being believed, and of course the safe, loving and supportive relationships Jo has built with her family and friends.

I thank Jo for her courage and generosity in sharing her story. I hope that the next chapter of Jo's story includes a sense of pride and satisfaction in knowing that in doing so, she has helped many others. I also hope the next chapter includes a sense of pride for all she has overcome, and that the compassion Jo holds for others extends to herself. Most of all, I hope the next chapter brings enough joy and positive experiences for Jo to finally believe that she can "trust happy".

Lisa M.

Manager, Sexual Assault Service

A note from Jo

Hello! I assume that if you have picked up my book, we have something in common.

I see you.

One or more situations you've experienced have caused you to be trapped in a life of numerous emotional, mental or physical wounds and malfunctions. Depending on your age group, the way you have dealt with, or not dealt with, these dysfunctions will have had a tremendous impact on you. Dysfunction will dictate how you perform in a society that sometimes seems void of empathy for individuals like us who have suffered trauma at the hands of another person.

My story began in the 1950s. This was a time when society's awkwardness and fear relating to anything that happened behind closed doors was deemed taboo, off limits and nobody's business but those living the abuse. I have not held back in my recollections, so be sure that you have the support you need around you if my story brings up memories from your own past.

Men of that time were allowed, sometimes even encouraged, to be cruel towards their families. A firm hand and an abusive tongue were accepted as normal. My life changed forever when a man who was supposed to protect me from harm caused irreparable damage to me physically and emotionally. He abused his position of trust with my family to do whatever he wanted to the body and soul of a helpless toddler and continued his practice for years.

A couple of very close friends I grew up with were the only people privy to my abuse. It was only when the accumulation of trauma, triggers and tears became too much for me to bear any longer that I was able to push through my crippling fear to disclose. I was 60 years old and broken. I had to widen my trust circle and allow medical professionals to help me.

A lifetime of trying to understand the person I was, why I was different and why I wasn't coping, took a tremendous toll on my emotional, mental, physical and spiritual health.

If you are part of the older generation, please know that it is never too late to seek professional help. *Never*. Today's society is open and willing to listen, accept and encourage healing from historical traumas.

Because I kept my secrets for over 60 years, it is not an easy road for me to heal because memories of my abuse are firmly embedded in every cell of my body. It hasn't been easy to spill my guts, as they say, to complete strangers. To be honest and forthcoming without the fear of ridicule or punishment for speaking out has been overwhelming. I have learnt a lot about myself, though. Why I react to situations. How to help myself through those situations. Tools of the trade, you might say.

We all have a backstory. No matter the extent of our backstory, or what generation we were born into, we are all entitled to be believed, informed, nurtured and accepted.

Many different characters have appeared in my true-life story. Some have scared me, some have taken my innocence, some have suppressed me, some have emotionally hurt me beyond comprehension, and some have tried their best to comfort me. Characters both good and bad have been relatives, people in authority, so-called friends, professionals and dear friends. The many adversities throughout my lifetime have left me afflicted by shame, hatred of self and others, exhaustion, confusion, anxiety, depression and in later life being diagnosed with Complex Post-Traumatic Stress Disorder (CPTSD) and Dissociative Identity Disorder (DID, also known as Multiple Personality Disorder).

The years go by and more traumas occur, and *still* I do not tell. I suffer horrifically through silence. I grow up emotionally and mentally wounded. I am left to my own, sometimes very ineffective, devices to deal with the ongoing, out-of-control fallout of emotions and overwhelming pain caused by my traumas. As a result of my abuses and not receiving informative counselling early, I do not trust, and I haven't been taught how to be present in my own life. As I grew into an adult, my childhood traumas were well and truly cemented into my being.

The traumas I have endured throughout my lifetime have left a very disturbing residue of emotions and responses. This residue has affected my every waking moment as well as causing me to have a disturbed sleep pattern.

When I was a child, the family structure was very different. A family member *never* spoke of situations that may have developed behind closed doors. In other words, we *never* aired the family's "dirty laundry" in public. Secrets were kept, facades were put up to hide realities, and those in authority just didn't want to know.

As I write this, I am on the cusp of my 70th birthday, and I still do not know who I am. You may ask, "How come you don't know who you are?" It is a valid and meaningful question. One I have asked myself time and time again throughout my life. One I would be so grateful to know the true answers to. My life has been complicated and hard to come to terms with at times.

I have had characters scattered throughout my life's journey who have enveloped me in love, happiness, laughter and peace. Unfortunately, some characters have betrayed, abused and made me question whether my life was worth living.

My emotional self is tired from trying to accommodate the array of feelings that have been both my friend and my enemy as the years have gone by.

Was my being diagnosed with DID the way I coped with the many adversities throughout my life? Adversity can be thrust upon us, manifested by ourselves or perpetrated by those who wish gratification for themselves. *How does that look in a person's life? What are the repercussions of adversity? Can that be explained simply?* Can adversity be bundled into one category, or do we have to break it down into the different types of adversity?

Adversity in my life looks like child sexual abuse, domestic violence and a traumatic car crash. These adversities are a few of the traumas that entered my life. The unforgettable memories resulting from these traumas have stayed with me, causing immeasurable damage to my wellbeing.

What techniques does one use to overcome, to thrive and to try and forgive through adversity? In my case, as I grew up, it was just trial and error, trying to find ways to help myself through the many debilitating panic attacks, exhausting depressive episodes and extremely negative thought patterns, so that I could live and not just shut myself off.

Memories are complicated and multilayered. Are our memories truth or fiction? Are they child's play or adult whimsy? Are memories supposed to be energetic or just static? Are they supposed to be frightening? Are they supposed to be happy and full of wonderment? Would you describe a memory as being an answer to a question? Or do you feel a memory is its own story waiting to be told? Maybe a story of deceit? Maybe a fictional story full of wonder and excitement? A long-lost yearning for the truth? Or simply a fanciful version of an event?

Whatever your thoughts are on memories, if the traumatic memories are left undealt with, they will ravage your body on every level, through overwhelming negative emotions such as stress and self-hatred. These memories will also torture the mind until one may try to create a quick exit from their agonising existence by numerous suicide attempts. I know – I have lived it. I have many traumatic memories. I also have no recollection of many events that have happened, both good and bad, all the way through my life. I question if these known and unknown memories are supposed to be told or hidden forever.

I have had many questions I wanted answers to over time. Some more complex than others. Some questions were brought about by mistreatment and pain. Some questions as I got older were directed to me, to my mentality, to my hatred of self and others, to my wanting to know why I am the way I am. Why I felt I was so different to other people. I questioned those in authority and power. Some questions were even directed towards those adults who were supposed to protect me.

I hated not knowing why happiness was so hard for me to achieve. I had forgotten how to smile.

Who am I? I know that I am a daughter, sister, mother, wife, grandmother and great-grandmother. They are things that have just happened. They are beautiful things, wonderful things. To be all those things is awesome. To have given life and to see that life birth another generation and then another is mind-blowing. I love my family with all my heart. To the moon and back, as the saying goes. I have an amazing relationship with my children and grandchildren, and I am so grateful for the part that each one has played in my life. The unconditional love and support I have received has kept me coming back from the overwhelming precipice that I have almost stepped off many times throughout my life.

But who else am I? Am I a writer? Am I a painter? Am I a sculptor? Am I a student? Or am I just a homebody?

I have absolutely no idea. Because from two years old, my life was not my own.

My message throughout my book is: no matter how old you are, male or female or other, rich or poor, black, white or brindle, religious or not religious, spiritual or not spiritual, it is never too late to seek professional help for abuse. Any sort of abuse, emotional, mental, physical or spiritual, is *not* okay.

If you have been abused and you haven't told anyone, and perhaps feel overwhelmed by emotions and mental health conditions you don't understand, seek professional help.

You deserve to be heard, to be helped and ultimately healed.

I see you and you've got this.

Jo

CHAPTER 1

My inner child

My heart is heavy, my soul is still dying
This life on Earth, I cannot stop crying
I have thoughts of heaven, is there such a place?
I think of myself as a waste of space

Help I seek, but from what direction?
I am told by some, "Stop seeking perfection"
Others may say, "Drugs you do need
That will help numb your withering seed"

But in my mind, if my seed dies
Then taking my life is what before me lies
There must be something more fulfilling ahead
than a life full of suffering, and to be dead

Your family and friends have heaps to say
Your thoughts turn to God, "Please help me" you pray
His words come to you, "Turn inwards, my child"
You have heard this before; it only makes you wild

You shout at this God, "I don't understand"
Where will I find such a helping hand?
"Turn inwards, my child", you hear it again
Your tears start to fall, you are riddled with pain

The love you once felt has gone from your heart
The seed that once grew has been torn apart
The child that was once so carefree and gay
is now no more than an empty day

You start to think of the child who used to be
This child in your mind, this child you can see
You remember the laughter, the joy and the love
That came from this child, this child from above

"Turn inwards, my child", the words keep on saying
"Please send help from above", you keep on praying
You see in your mind the family you adore
Can you give them the love you once did before?

You are frightened by the feelings that are stirring inside
Will you be hurt like before and again seek to hide?
You pray for the strength and wisdom you need
To reopen your heart and plant a new seed

"Turn inwards, my child" you see the white light
You thank God for the calmness, which is now in your sight
How long has it been since you felt peace and love?
"One day at a time" is your message from above

Your prayers are all answered, your faith is restored
Loving thoughts fill your days, you are no longer gored
As you and your inner child become one again
The words "I love you" will always remain

—Jo Wilcox

2015

Will the doctor be much longer? I don't think I can go through with this. The mental gremlins are working overtime, trying to get me to pick up sticks and leave before I spill my secrets to the doctor. *This is our secret. You mustn't tell anyone. If you do, I will hurt your sisters.* I have held these secrets quietly and carefully, always aware of the frightening circumstances if I accidentally let my guard down and blab.

I am at my wits' end. The gremlins in my head are always feeding me bullshit. *You are no good, you will never amount to anything, you are not clever enough.* Belittling words and negative thoughts run around in my head, on a constant loop. It is like waves crashing against the shore, never letting up. With each pounding, a small piece of my sanity is washed away.

The last few weeks have been dreadful. The events and my reactions to them have brought me to my doctor's waiting room. I am a screaming mess, literally. My anger, self-hatred, self-sabotage and sense of hopelessness are my constant companions. Pushing me deeper into the torturous black hole that has been my abuser for over 60 years. No matter how hard I try and claw myself out of this nightmare, the triggers of my past are a constant reminder that my present day-to-day world has no power over my past.

My doctor appears and calls my name. As I follow her nervously down the familiar hallway, I agonise about what she will say. *Will she believe me? Will she just say it is all in my head, give me a pill and send me on my way?* It only takes a minute to arrive at my doctor's room. My anxiety is through the roof and my imagination is illuminated, and not in a good way. All I can think is: *if I tell, my sisters will be hurt.* My past has again come back to spit in my face. It is unsettling how much my mind will betray me when I am in a heightened state of panic.

My mind is not my friend. It is a relentless dictator of all things scary.

My life has been one big scare fest, which I have been unwittingly shackled to. *Will the day ever come when I can remove these shackles and step off the roundabout of self-hatred, self-loathing and self-sabotage?*

I start to doubt myself. *Do I have the strength to go through with this?* I have lived this way all my life. The intense anger, the debilitating panic attacks, the demoralising negative self-talk and the suicide attempts have emptied my positive energy bucket, and I do not see my bucket being filled any time soon.

My doctor beckons for me to have a seat. *Oh crap.* My bum only just touches the seat, and a truckload of words fall out of my mouth.

"I am not allowed to tell you, but I have to."

"What do you mean you are not allowed to tell me? Tell me what, Jo?" My doctor is puzzled and I don't blame her.

I am rambling, confused, trying desperately to string words together in a cohesive way.

"He will hurt my sisters if I tell anyone. He will *hurt* them. Don't you understand that? It is a secret. No. No. I cannot tell you."

I start to stand up. I am going to leave this claustrophobic room, run away.

"Jo, it is okay. Sit down, Jo. You can tell me anything. I want to help you."

"I was sexually abused when I was little. He hurt me. He scared me. I hate him." My heart is pounding, fear ready to consume me. Ready to eat me alive.

"Who hurt you? You can tell me, Jo. It is okay – I will help you. Who hurt you, Jo?"

The tears I have not allowed to flow are cascading down my face, leaving small wet dots on my blouse. My doctor passes me the tissue box as she calmly reassures me.

"My step-grandfather. I hate him. He hurt me."

"Oh, Jo, I am so sorry. It will be okay. Are you able to tell me a little bit about what happened?"

I have no idea if I am making any sense. My emotions are out of control as I try desperately to gather my thoughts and control my flow of tears. I start to, hopefully coherently, tell my doctor my story of abuse and betrayal.

"Can you help me if I tell the truth and tell you what happened a couple of days ago? Can you help me?"

I proceed to recount the events that led me to be sitting, scared out of my wits, in my doctor's room.

It was a school day, and I was to pick up my grandkids and take them to school. I loved, loved, loved being with them. That morning, I felt triggered, emotionally and mentally helpless, extremely agitated and angry. My feeling of hopelessness was overwhelming. Many times over the years, I never had any idea why I would suddenly go into a recurring loop of fear.

I drove out of my driveway, thinking that seeing Hannah, Oscar and Archie would brighten my mood. My mind was playing out the never-ending self-ridicule that filled my waking day. The constant barrage of horrendous flashbacks and memories of abuse flooded in. I could see only one way out.

Up ahead, a sharp bend provided an opportunity. Directly in front of the bend was a solid mass of gum trees, standing like soldiers, ready to capture the unexpected if it ventured too close to their domain. In the few short seconds before rounding the bend, I ask myself: *do I wish to live or die? Is my third suicide attempt looming? Maybe I will succeed this time...*

My frustration with life and myself had grown like a grotesque malignancy. Thoughts of my two amazing kids, Kylie and Guy, caused my heart to flutter. I realised that all the trials and tribulations in the entire universe would not deplete the love I have for, and receive from, those two precious individuals.

Tears tumbled down my face as I gathered speed. My mind was made up.

Today will be my last day on this unrelenting, uncompromising, unloving planet. Then all of a sudden, through my tear-soaked eyes I saw my grandson Archie's smiling face in front of me. His loving eyes were looking at me. He spoke to me: "Grandma, I love you." I was jolted out of my suicidal stupor just in time to fling the steering wheel to follow the curve of the road. The gum trees lost out this time.

Whether you believe in divine intervention or not, I do not tell a lie. Archie just saved my life. I have so much love for my grandkids and I know they love me with all their hearts, too.

My mind was racing. I was crying, screaming and utterly exhausted. I pulled over on the side of the road, shaking uncontrollably. Only seconds had past, but it felt like a lifetime. My world felt so unreal. *Am I having a mental breakdown?* I couldn't take too much time to compose myself as I was on my way to pick up my grandkids to take them to school. I thought about how I could conceal my emotion and come across as my normal self. *Well, that is an oxymoron. There has never been anything normal about me.*

So, with my sunglasses on, hiding my red bulging eyes, and with a big smile on my face, I drove off. I greeted my amazing grandkids with hugs and kisses. On the way to school, we laughed and chatted about their day ahead. Another round of big hugs and kisses as I dropped the grandkids off. Driving away, I could finally fall apart. Crying uncontrollably, I tried to process what had happened.

Sitting in my doctor's room telling her this story, I was once again in tears and feeling very humbled by my life-altering experience. My story had amazed and horrified her at the same time.

A few months earlier, I had told my doctor about the domestic violence in my home during my childhood. She wanted me to see a psychiatrist, but I refused. This was the first time I'd uttered a single word about the sexual abuse to a professional.

I could still hear *him*, my step-grandfather, whispering in my ear, "If you tell anyone, I will hurt your sisters." Those words left such a deep scar; *nothing* would make me tell a professional. I had handled life by myself up until then. I didn't need any help. But after my third suicide attempt, I understood the severity of my mental health issues. I knew deep in my heart that I needed help. *I have to trust the process.*

There is no roadmap to follow when it comes to surviving trauma. What might work for one person may not work for another. We all do the best we can with the help of family, friends and whatever information we can get our hands on. What happens when the traumas start at a young age, are not spoken about and are not dealt with? They become a cruel and manipulative secret that grows, festers and strangles the mind, body and soul of the abused.

When I eventually sought professional help, the years of dealing with life's absurdities on my own made accepting help feel as foreign as seeing pigs fly. Mistrust swirled around every word a professional uttered. Vulnerability became my most feared enemy. I no longer recognised myself. I was no longer the person I grew up as. I had not yet become the person I had always dreamed of being, healed and happy. Trying to exist in the middle of the two extremes only brought more pain and suffering. "I am scared shitless but I cannot do this on my own anymore" had become my new catchcry.

Emotional upheaval and mental exhaustion accompanied every word I spoke that day I disclosed the abuse to my doctor. My body shook as the captured destructive energy started to be released.

I have always agonised about why I felt so broken, different, and unable to be happy and just "be" in my life. I couldn't see any way out of my misery. My past hurts and abuses had taken up residence in my fragile body and mind permanently. Nothing made sense anymore. As I had done many times before, I put on a brave, happy façade. No one knew the destructive emotional turmoil I was suffering.

Stepping through the veil of invisibility that shrouded me all my life, to tell my story, left me frightened initially.

I wasn't sure if I had done the right thing. I felt like I had betrayed myself and my own safety. *Why did I do this? Why did I put myself in harm's way? You were told what would happen if you told.* My step-grandfather's words haunted me.

Every emotion, every cell in my body, had been set alight. I was on fire. The vulnerability I was feeling fuelled my exhaustion. Meanwhile, the relief of unburdening myself, knowing that my doctor believed and positively acknowledged every word I told her, was priceless for me. *My doctor heard me, she believed me. Shit – she really believed me.*

Walking back to my car after my appointment, tissues in hand, I started to feel a little calmer. I had taken the first step. Thoughts invaded my already troubled mind, skipping forward into my unknown future, backward into my abusive past and then forward into my scary present. *Will I have to tell my story all over again to other people? I don't think I can do that. I cannot do this on my own.*

I no longer had the strength to keep going on my own. It was time to break the silence.

An appointment was made to see a psychiatrist. My doctor also put me on suicide watch. I had an organisation ring me every day. It drove me nuts. Their intentions were pure – they only wanted to help me and keep my safe. I was so used to doing everything on my own. Paddling my own canoe – for better or worse – I couldn't relate to people wanting to help me. I was 60 years old. It was a long time to fend for myself.

I started to realise it is my job as a trauma survivor to seek help from family, friends and health professionals. It is my job to nurture my wounds, listen to my inner child and go easy on myself. It is my job to reveal my secrets and, where possible, seek justice for my suffering. It is my job to become the keeper of self-love, self-forgiveness and self-growth. I may not be as I was born, innocent and pure. But I owe it to myself to never stop fighting for my dignity. Fighting to have the right to speak up and be believed, along with being shrouded in happiness and peace for the rest of my life.

My psychiatrist was a lovely lady who was hoping I would be able to tolerate antidepressants. I remember trying a few different types, although none had the desired effect. My symptoms were getting worse. My depression wouldn't let up. Suicidal thoughts were a constant worry. Episodes of extreme hopelessness were overtaking my life. She even got my husband to come in for an appointment so she could explain to him my mental health issues in a manner he may understand. Eventually, my psychiatrist told me that if I didn't improve, she would have me admitted to hospital.

In my mind, these words were not a comfort – they were a threat. My immediate response was: *I won't be going to hospital.* My emotional whirlpool of emotions was being stirred up, memories of being trapped consumed me. After decades of not knowing, I was now privy to my own mentality and I didn't like it.

After a number of visits to my psychiatrist, I was sent to have sexual abuse counselling. Another new person to tell my story to. *This is becoming exhausting.* However, it only took a few sessions for me to trust my counsellor. I opened up about the self-harm episodes I had experienced. I was told they were called Deliberate Self-harm (DSH). Until she explained what can cause self-harm, I just chalked it up to another unknown paradox in my life.

I questioned myself constantly. *Why had I become the person I was? Why do I do the things I do? Why do I not remember doing certain things or being in certain places?* These were disturbing situations sometimes, but I thought: *that is just how it is. I am just a no-good waste of space and deserve all the abuse and mistreatment I receive.* Most damagingly, I minimised and even trivialised my experiences. *These things happened to other people as well. It is just life. Stop your grumbling.*

My counselling sessions were enlightening. I was given extensive information on the ramifications of child sexual abuse, including what it does to the growing infant brain. I didn't know that the person I had become, and the loss of memory, were symptoms, and that, no, not everyone was like me because not everyone was sexually abused as a child.

CHAPTER 2

How can I find her?

She is nowhere and everywhere
She is alive, but she is dead
An empty shell
Yearning to be fulfilled
Happiness eludes her
Misery surrounds her
Her fortress is secure
Walls high and mighty
Her resolve strong
Forever unforgiving
Weakness is her enemy
Silence, her keeper
Where is she now?
She flits from place to place
Unrecognisable, unassuming
Her disguise well worn
Lost forever, she cannot be found

—Jo Wilcox

The earliest memory of my child sexual abuse is when I was about two years old. I was standing up in my cot, holding onto the side. A large man was hovering over me, smiling and talking lovingly. I remember smiling back, feeling happy and content. The man was my mum's stepfather. He was a tall man with a bald head, and he wore glasses.

His hands were caressing me gently. After a short time, his hands moved from my arms to my tummy and then to the front of my nappy. His next move was to place his hand inside my nappy and touch my private parts. I do not remember this experience upsetting me. It is just something I remember.

This ritual happened many times when I was still in nappies and may have happened to me at a younger age, but I do not remember. Now, you may say, "How could this small child remember this? She is making it all up." All I can say is that I have had this memory for as long as I can remember. I thought nothing of it over the years. Mainly because for a long time I didn't know that what my step-grandfather was doing to me was wrong.

I was the only child at the time and my parents didn't tell me when my step-grandfather was coming to visit. He would just arrive. My step-grandfather was very attentive. We would play special games. Even when my younger sister, Lisa, was born, followed by my youngest sister, Susie, when I was five, these games were only for him and me to play.

I felt very special and of course I knew I was my step-grandfather's favourite. I was too young to realise this man was a predator and a manipulator.

Preying on a small child to fulfil his sexual depravity. I hated hearing him say, "Now, this is our little secret. You mustn't tell anyone."

As I am writing this, my mind hesitantly goes back to when I was a child. My grandmother, my mum's mum, was a seamstress. A beautiful sewer. She made me and my sisters beautiful little dresses. I adored my little dresses – the way they swished when I moved from side to side. I felt like a princess when I wore them and was so happy. How beautiful I looked, colourful and carefree.

One day, my family had gone out together, all dressed up. We arrived home, all of us happy and laughing after having a wonderful time. In a millisecond, my happiness was shattered by the presence of my step-grandfather standing in front of me when I got out of the car. He was so happy to see me.

"Hello, Jo. You look so beautiful, like an adorable little doll. I love your pretty dress. Come here so I can give you a big hug in your beautiful dress."

My world shattered into millions of little pieces as this man's hands invaded my personal space. His breath quickening with each hug he gave me.

My step-grandfather stayed for a few days, which meant secret times together. He would tell my parents we were going to play. He would take my hand and lead me anywhere that was secluded enough that he could abuse his power over me. On one particular day we were all going out, again dressed in our finest. Me and my sisters looking so special in our little dresses. Step-grandfather wanted me to stay home with him. So, he made up some excuse. I was only little – I had no power or say over the situation.

Each time he visited, I was a little bit older. I wasn't really happy doing the things that step-grandfather wanted me to do. My gut was telling me: *something isn't right. I don't want to do this. I don't want to stay home. I want to go with my mum and dad.* On one occasion, I waved goodbye to everyone, while holding step-grandfather's hand. He led me back inside the house, sat me down on the lounge, his looming frame towering over me. He proceeded to take off my shoes and socks. I had the cutest pair of little socks. They were pink and had little frills on the top. They were my favourite. My beautiful little dress was the next to be removed and then my undies. All the while he was telling me how pretty I was, that I was his favourite, and of course the words that were etched into my brain, never to be removed: "Now, this is our little secret. You mustn't tell anyone."

As he was removing his trousers and underpants, while standing in front of me, I wondered: *what would he like me to do this time?* He had all the time in the world to fulfil his yucky desires. He gathered up all the clothes strewn on the floor, took my hand, and led me into my bedroom. I do not remember ever having intercourse with him, but because of my DID and the number of different parts I have, it may have happened. Maybe a part is still holding that memory, keeping it hidden way back in my memory train. It would have been too traumatic for me to cope with while it was happening. My parts value my safety at all costs.

He caressed my tiny body, spread my legs and penetrated my vagina with his fingers. I remember his penis standing up again like other times, and how he placed my little shaking hand on it and made me lick it. All this time I wished Mum and Dad would come home. It wasn't long before the smelly, sticky goo was all over my tummy. He helped me have a shower and get dressed. I understand why now. There couldn't be any trace that there had been any foul play going on while Mum and Dad were away. Mum, Dad and my sisters came home a couple of hours later.

Of course, I had learnt what to do. I smiled, said hello and played with my sisters, as though nothing had happened.

As I got older and the sexual abuse continued, the games we played upset me. The secrets I had to keep made me feel that I was being naughty. I started to realise that what we were doing wasn't right.

He could sense I wasn't happy with his game. I was wary and uneasy being his plaything. To combat this, he started to tell me, "Now, this is our little secret. If you tell anyone, I will hurt your sisters." I didn't want my sisters to be hurt so I stayed compliant. A few more years went by and step-grandfather's visits and interest in me decreased. His visits finally stopped. I don't remember how old I was when the abuse stopped but I was so relieved.

In among all of this, I have happy childhood memories of growing up with my sisters. We lived in the city until I was in Year Three, at which point my family and I moved to the country. Our home in the city backed onto a railway track. An enormous tree with large dangling limbs sat proudly in the backyard. I would climb this tree as high as my young age would allow me, watching the puffing billies, as they were called back then, go past as I clung tightly to my precarious vantage point. Thick smoke billowed from the smokestack of the train as it chugged along the track.

Running away from home – taking our small black dog, Kimmy, with me – was my thing. I would dress her up in old clothes before putting her in my little doll pram. We would go on adventures together all the time. I would walk out the front gate and down the footpath, pushing her along while she sat, enjoying the ride. When she wanted to get out of the pram, she would walk beside me. We would get to the corner, but she wouldn't cross the road. So my running away from home ended at the corner. I would turn around and walk back home. I ran away so often that Mum resorted to tying me to the clothesline. Better safe than sorry.

I wonder sometimes: *is my life based on memories? Am I defined by my memories? Why is it that my not-so-nice memories are the ones that seem to take the front seat, in the front carriage of my memory train? Is the trauma manifested by these horrific memories too powerful, too easy to access because they are in the front?* I would love my life to be filled with happy, carefree and colourful memories. Unfortunately, that is not always the case.

I don't wear makeup. I wear pants and shirts. I wear my hair short and grey, so I don't stand out. So, I am not noticed. I own one dress. Yes, one. And I only wear it when I absolutely have to. Otherwise, I always dress down. I am always neat, tidy and clean, but as inconspicuous as I can be. This is the aftermath of being abused by my step-grandfather while I was wearing my beautiful little dress and my pretty pink socks with the little frills.

I told myself: if I am not pretty, I won't get hurt. If I am not happy, I won't get hurt.

I started school when I was just five years old. Looking back now, I was too young. I hated being in the school environment. There were too many people at school. It was scary. I had to be in a classroom with a man I didn't know. I couldn't leave if I wanted to. I was trapped. I used to run away from school also. The only time I felt happy at school was at lunch, when I was free to play with other kids or be on my own if I wanted to.

A memory has surfaced from when I was in Year Two. I was playing with an older girl. We were jumping over the long bench seats underneath the school buildings during lunch time. She was pulling me along, but my little legs couldn't go as fast or jump as high as hers. *Splat*. I ended up face down on the cement. I was six years old. The area between my upper lip and my nose was split, blood gushing everywhere. Mum came and took me to the doctor. I was crying and very scared. Mum and I were ushered into a very scary-looking room. I saw all these terrifying, shiny things that resembled knives and forks. By this time, I was hysterical. A man I had never seen before came towards me, wanting to touch me. My hysteria turned into sheer terror. *Is this man going to hurt me? I won't let him touch me.*

I had to have stitches for the split. This meant I had to lay still and allow people to touch me. *No way, José*. I was only little, but it took three grown adults to hold me down so the doctor could stitch me up. The whole time lying on the table, being held down, feeling so horribly vulnerable, all I could think was: *they are going to hurt me*. Yes, they did. Needles pushed unceremoniously into my little face and then I was stitched up like a hessian bag. I still have the scar where I was traumatically repaired.

Who do you think you are? You aren't good enough to do anything! You are a waste of space. You won't succeed – you are too stupid. Go back into your bedroom and draw – that is all you are good for.

My childhood wasn't easy. My father was cruel at times, but he also had his good qualities. He was loving. He loved hugs. He always said good morning. I always got a goodnight kiss before I went to bed. He played games with my younger sisters and me when we were kids. He provided well for his family. We always had food, clothing and a roof over our heads.

Unfortunately, my father found rum. He was a totally different person when he drank rum. He was sarcastic, angry, relentlessly controlling and terrifying. My father never physically hit me, but his sarcasm was brutal. He left me feeling like a worthless piece of shit many, many times. A loving family man destroyed by alcohol.

Friday night was pub night. My job was to make sure my two younger sisters and I were showered and dressed appropriately after we got home from school. At five o'clock, we would walk down to the pub to meet our parents. They ran their own business and would go to the pub after they closed up. It was not a place for children back then.

My father's continuous tirade of put-downs and belittling criticisms rang out in my head like a church bell summoning its devout subjects to prayer. Year after year as I grew up, I had my father in my head. I was his devotee. I was his whipping horse. I was the one he went to when he wanted to feel powerful and in control. Being the eldest child was a burden.

I had no control over anything in my life growing up. Being told, "Do this, go here, stand up, sit down." There was one thing I did to have some sense of control. It may seem small and trivial now, but back then – when I was living in a whirlwind of unpredictability and fear – it was heaven to me.

When we all sat at the table to have dinner, I would survey my plate, noticing all the different food groups. Meat, potato, pumpkin, peas and gravy. No matter what the array of nourishment was, I deliberately separated each food group so none of my food touched. I ate each pile on its own. I sat there pleased as punch, smiling on the inside, imagining I was sending a royal *up yours* to Dad.

Being blamed for everything that went on in my father's world was hurtful, tremendously soul-destroying and exhausting. Hurtful because my fragile ego was forever bombarded with negative dialogue, causing low self-esteem. Tremendously soul-destroying because every day my young life force was being sucked from my physical body. Exhausting because I very rarely felt safe. Not knowing what mood my father may be in – drunk, sober, happy or angry – was torturous.

A small child cannot grow up normally when they hardly sleep and are constantly hypervigilant.

CHAPTER 3

Confusion

I am invisible
But I want to be seen
I am mute
But I want to be heard
I am untouchable
But I want to be touched
I am numb
But I want to feel
Why is there doubt
When there could be clarity?
Why is there anger
When there could be peace?
Why is there sadness
When there could be happiness?
Why is there hopelessness
When there could be inspiration?
My mind is the creator of good and evil
My mind is also the creator of hatred and love
There is no logical answer to the torment
known by the one who is burdened
There is only the confusion

—Jo Wilcox

Throughout my developmental years, I wasn't always nurtured or supported. I wasn't given the opportunities to pursue my dreams or desires. Adults who were supposed to encourage me were unable to do so. In my adult years, I have come to understand why these adults acted as they did. They too had backstories that led them to be who they were. What were their backstories? What caused them to be so disconnected?

I truly believe that if trauma is your yardstick for growing up, then it will follow you into adulthood unless you can access professional help early.

I wasn't afforded access to early professional intervention. The same scenario, lack of professional help, was also my parents' downfall.

When I was in my forties, I started looking into my family genealogy. I was keen to find out where my ancestors came from. I spent hours researching before having to purchase heaps of birth, death and marriage certificates so I could delve further back into my lineage. An opportunity presented itself to ask my mum, dad and grandma (who was visiting at the time), questions about their lives. I started to tell my family that I was delving into our family tree. Well, based on the reaction I received from them all, you would have thought I was going to line them all up against a wall and shoot them.

My father was the first one to tell me in no uncertain terms to "back off". I had no idea what I had done wrong, why my questions were so intrusive, and why it seemed like my ancestry was to be buried and never talked about again. I was accused of wanting to dig up long-lost secrets and divulge them to anyone who would listen. I was hurt to think that my family thought so little of me. But that is what fear will do to you. Fear that your secrets will be found out.

My mother was born out of wedlock in 1929, after my grandma had an affair with a married man. Shock horror? No. But back then, it was unthinkable and incredibly frowned upon. I didn't love my mother any less. I didn't disrespect my grandma because of this revelation. Once everyone realised that it was okay, after a few weeks I was allowed to ask questions about my history.

This revelation helped me to finally understand why Mum was so shutdown emotionally. Grandma stayed at an unmarried women's hostel and worked for her keep until Mum was born. Mum's father's relatives wanted to take Mum and raise her as their own. Grandma wouldn't have it. But she also didn't want to have anything to do with Mum. Grandma's mother and father raised Mum for the first seven years of her life. They then told Grandma that she had to take Mum back and raise her.

This was the worst thing that could have happened to Mum. As she grew up, she was shuttled from house to house, relative to relative. You could imagine the abandonment issues Mum had, the worthlessness she must have felt, with no one wanting her.

Dad's mum, my nana, was a beautiful, loving lady. Her husband, my pop, served in World War II, leaving Nana with two sons to care for on her own. My dad was 10 years older than his younger brother, so a lot of the care fell to him. How traumatic it must have been for Dad to see his father off to war. No emails or mobile phone calls to keep in touch. Just a written letter posted. Waiting months for a reply. Never knowing if he was dead or alive.

Pop was given a medical discharge from the army. He died before I was born. The emotional impact of both Mum and Dad's early lives would have been immense. Back in the 1920s, 30s and 40s, there weren't many mental health professionals to help. No diagnoses of Post-Traumatic Stress Disorder (PTSD), no understanding of what childhood trauma looked like. You just got on with it. Your lot was your lot.

With Mum's childhood being what it was, she didn't need her mother to hook up with someone like my step-grandfather. As I explored the family genealogy, I found out that this horror of a man had more than one name. In fact, he had a number of aliases. I have the official documents to prove it. He also tried to abuse my mum when she was in her teens. Mum asked her uncle to come and put a lock on her bedroom door to stop him. Finding out this piece of information later in my life helped me to understand why my mum was the way she was.

When my sisters and I had young families of our own, Mum would sometimes stay upstairs when we came to visit and not participate. She was very guarded. I am sure she had undiagnosed depression, anxiety and PTSD.

My parents projected their negative upbringings on to me. Even though I understand to some extent the victimisation I received from these adults, it's still hard to reckon with. I grapple with the fact that they didn't want to be different from their parents and show me the loving and uplifting childhood, teenage and even adult years I am sure they wanted to receive from their parents. Instead, the generational abuse continued. They chose to become victims themselves. They turned to alcohol as their savour. I am sure Mum and Dad were both undiagnosed alcoholics.

Oh! My head hurts. I feel dizzy. What happened? I look around and see. *Oh no, oh no, oh no.* Susie is lying on the floor of the car, half under the car seat. *Is she dead?* I am so scared, I am trapped, I cannot get out. *What happened?* I hear screaming and crying. *Is that me? It is in my head...no...it is outside my head. She is not moving.* I can see Lisa sitting in the front seat, directly in front of me. She is bleeding, crying and screaming. She is trying to get out. I want to get out. But I can't. I am trapped. I want to get out. *Let me out. Let me out. My grandma...where is my grandma?*

I am panicking. *Oh no, there she is, sitting behind the wheel. She is really hurt, her arms don't look right.* Grandma cannot move – she cannot use her arms. I see other people now. They are trying to get Grandma out of the car. Someone helps Lisa get out. I look through the window – Lisa is crying, and she has blood on her beautiful dress. Her mouth is all bloody, she looks so scared. I cannot help her. I cannot get out. *Let me out. I want to get out.*

Only minutes have passed, but it feels like a lifetime. We have been involved in a car crash. There are people everywhere. *What is that dreadful noise?* It is hurting my ears. There is an ambulance. *Why is there an ambulance?* I am so scared. I push the front bucket seat forward and climb out of the car. Shaking uncontrollably, crying and dazed, I yell at people to get Susie out of the car.

"She is really hurt – help her! Get her out! Get her out!" *Why aren't people listening to me?* I try and go back to the car to get her out. They won't let me. Lisa and I are standing on the side of the footpath, crying hysterically.

It is 1967 and it is my 12th birthday. My sisters and I were visiting our grandma for the school holidays. We had flown down from Queensland to New South Wales unaccompanied. Our first flight on our own. We were travelling into town for my birthday celebration. My grandma had asked me if I wanted to wait for the mail to come or go straight into town. I don't remember which option I chose, but it was the wrong one. My belief all my life is that my decision resulted in us having a car crash. Back then, cars weren't fitted with seat belts. Grandma drove a small Triumph two-door sedan. We were hit by a much larger Holden four-door sedan. The driver had gone straight through a stop sign.

Ouch! I was shocked out of my hysterical state by a lady I didn't know slapping me and Lisa across the face. *What happened? What did I do wrong?*

"Stop crying!"

Living in the 60s was a nightmare. No compassion, no support – just hard, unemotional people.

Once they got Susie out of the car, she wouldn't get on the stretcher to be put in the ambulance. After a lot of reassurance from me, Susie, who was six-and-a-half years old, was placed into the ambulance along with Grandma, Lisa and myself. I remember being in the back of the ambulance with Susie – she wasn't breathing properly. I knew in my heart that there was something wrong. I yelled at the ambulance driver to go faster, but no one listened. It felt like we were going that slow that I could have walked faster to the hospital. When we arrived at the hospital, Susie was taken away, but I didn't know where. Grandma, Lisa and I were taken somewhere else altogether.

Because there were no seat belts, nine-year-old Lisa, who was in the front passenger seat, was thrown forward. As a result, she smashed her face on the dashboard, with her teeth and mouth sustaining damage. Lisa was so upset because blood from her broken mouth was on her pretty dress.

While we were waiting to be seen by the doctor, my grandma wanted a drink of water. I went off and brought back a glass of water for her. Unfortunately, my action resulted in my grandma not being treated for many more hours, causing her to endure the pain for a lot longer. My guilt was piling up.

Next thing, Susie's doctor came and asked me to help them with her. She was petrified and wouldn't allow them to undress her. I could see the terror in her little eyes. I did what I could to get her settled. Susie's breathing was dreadful. I was so scared for her. After I was taken back to Grandma and Lisa, the doctor came to see me again. He asked me, "Does your sister have a cold?" I was only 12 years old, but I was furious.

"I've been trying to tell you that there is something wrong! She can't breathe properly! No! She doesn't have a cold!" I yelled at the doctor. Of course, he raced off to then save Susie's life. Once the doctors knew she didn't have a cold, they performed numerous procedures and found out that Susie had a collapsed right lung caused by a rib compressing against it. That is called a pneumothorax. She also had a bowel haemorrhage. I was on my own, trying to deal with everything going on, being the adult, caring for everyone and hoping to keep everyone safe. I knew that with my parents in another state they wouldn't be able to help me for ages.

Both my sisters and my grandma came through this horrific ordeal. I didn't have a scratch on me from the crash. Once my parents arrived, I no longer had to deal with everything on my own, and I went into shock.

For years after the crash, each time I was in a car and had to drive through an intersection I would freak out. Car sickness travelled with me every time I got in a car. To this day, I will always drive, unless I am going with someone I trust. Then I will be a passenger.

Susie told me many years later that she remembers looking down at herself while she was being operated on. She was having an out-of-body experience. That horrific day almost took my youngest sister from me. I am forever grateful that we all survived a day that was supposed to be a celebration but ended up being a tragedy of mega proportions.

I was in Year Eight when we had the car crash. I was dealing with recurring shock, while both my sisters were dealing with their injuries. Lisa had many years of torturous dental sessions to correct the impact of the crash. Dentistry in the 1960s and 70s was not pleasurable at all for a little girl to endure, while Susie was healing from major surgery.

Guilt was my strange bedfellow, robbing me of sleep. My sisters' pain and suffering was my fault.

The transition from primary school to high school was stressful. My step-grandfather was no longer in the picture, so I only had my dad to contend with. School was brutal in the 1960s. Teachers used their students as target practice. Blackboard erasers went flying, thrown on numerous occasions as the teacher tried to knock out a student who was misbehaving. Or they would come along and see how high they could lift you off your chair by your ear lobe. Being sent to the principal's office wasn't just for a discussion. If you didn't leave the office with welts across your hands from the cane, you were lucky. I found it really hard to listen and stay focused at school. I had headaches constantly. No matter how hard I studied at home, I couldn't retain the information. I worried all the time.

It was made even worse by the bullying. I am sure they could tell I was broken and fair game. A girl at school had it in for me, calling me names and putting me down. I would think: *I have all this shit to go through at home. Now I have to put up with this girl destroying my school life as well?*

I had already suffered physical abuse from her in Year Five when she stabbed my hand with a sharp pencil. The teacher spoke to us and then we were sent to the principal. Once again I was punished for something that wasn't my fault. Receiving the cane isn't a pleasant memory.

After a number of months, I told Mum and Dad what was happening.

"I am being bullied at school. This girl is so dreadful. I cannot take it anymore. I want to hurt her."

I didn't receive a hug or emotional support. I was told, "You cannot touch her. You are not allowed to fight anyone. Just ignore her and she will go away. You are not to touch her in the school grounds, ever."

I remember one day I was especially out of it mentally, and her constant verbal mudslinging upset me dreadfully.

Being the dutiful daughter that I am, always doing what I am told, I waited until she left the school grounds. I was walking home with my girlfriend,

Julie. We followed her out of the school gate, along the footpath. *You can get her now, you are outside the school grounds.* I was so angry.

With the power of a speeding train, I lunged forward and hit her in the middle of her back. She squealed. By the time I walked home, as I did every day, her mother had rung my mother. I was in a spot of bother when I walked in the back door that afternoon. My parents were also summoned to the principal's office. Of course I was in more trouble. *I didn't start any of this, but it is always my fault. Always.*

> *A life of being bullied lends itself to feeling so broken and worthless that becoming the bully is the only logical answer for self-preservation.*

People throughout my younger life often called me a snob. I wasn't a snob – it was a coping mechanism. Looking back, I would have been struggling with anxiety and depression. Trusting people was not an option. *Keep quiet and distant, and you won't get hurt.*

Despite his unpredictability, my father had a loving side also. I was 14 years old, and all my girlfriends had already got their periods. I hadn't. I was devastated and was moping around the house. My father noticed my mood. He approached me on one of his sober days and we sat together on the lounge.

"What is wrong? You seem so sad."

"I haven't got my period yet. All my friends have. I will never have any children." I was overcome with emotion at the idea that I would never be a mother. My loving dad sat with me, comforted me and assured me that I *would* have children. This version of my dad I loved with all my heart. I wished it was the only version that existed. That moments like this would last forever.

You might ask, "Why didn't my mother talk to me or comfort me?" Unfortunately, my mother was a very hard, emotionless person.

Dad was funny and had a happy smile. He was a good singer and would, on occasion, burst out in song. He was also a marvellous dancer. I have beautiful, loving memories of dancing with my dad. We would smile and twirl around the floor with grace.

CHAPTER 4

Surrender

Surrender to the beauty
Allow the essence of life to penetrate your being
Feel the tantalising touch of Mother Nature
As she glides past you
Be part of the sea
As it gently caresses the sand
While dancing towards the shore
Allow every breath you take
To beckon you closer to your inner sanctum
To be part of the wonderment
It is to be part of the knowing
Calm your mind
Become the sea
Embrace every breath
And
Surrender to the beauty

—Jo Wilcox

I was only 14 years old at the end of 1969. But because I turned 15 before school started in 1970, I was legally able to leave school. Graduating Year Ten was my highest level of schooling. To my relief, I had passed all my subjects except French, which wasn't a huge concern for me.

Growing up I had many wishes, big and small, some for the future, and some for the present. Wishing to have a future just for me when I left school was my ultimate goal as I grew up. My wish holder was a black cat soft toy. She comforted me while I was trying to hide from my life and listened to me when I was wishing for my dreams to come true. Wishes of safety, wishes of love, wishes of belonging and wishes of a happy future all melted away the older I got. Wishes of getting away from my family, going on to senior school, going to art school, were abandoned when my father had his wishes come true instead of mine. I wasn't allowed to leave town. My life after Year Ten was to work for my father in his business.

Like wishing on a star, one day
I will find my twinkle twinkle.

I do not remember if my father gave me a reason for his decision. Today I wonder whether it is because he just likes to control everyone or perhaps it is a leftover coping mechanism from his youth when his father went off to war. Did he think he would never see me again? Did he have to protect me like he did his baby brother while his dad was at war?

Smoke, I can smell smoke. Where is it coming from? I sit up, still half asleep, and look around through hazy eyes. The smoke is coming from the floor. *Oh shit.* Back in the 60s and 70s, not too many houses had fly screens or air conditioning. We definitely didn't. So, to combat the unbearably hot and sultry nights, which mosquitoes loved, the family used mosquito coils. If I was lucky, the pesky mosquitoes would keep their distance and I wouldn't be doing the "Aussie slap and wave away" to stop being bitten while trying to sleep.

The annoying buzzing drove me mad. My mosquito coil was normally on my desk, allowing the smoke to waft across me while I lay in bed. This night I was having a lot of trouble. There seemed to be a swarm of mosquitoes, so I decided to place the mosquito coil on the floor and allow the smoke to travel up instead of past me. I lit the mosquito coil, placed it on the floor, watched where the smoke was travelling, and thought: *yes, that is good*. Only, I was woken later in the night by smoke. I had two pillows and one had fallen off my bed onto the lit mosquito coil.

Holy crap! Thoughts of being burnt to death flood my mind. I am two storeys up, so I can't jump to safety. *Will my sisters be okay? I have to tell Mum and Dad.* I quietly walk to my parents' bedroom and stand next to my father's bed (Mum and Dad had separate beds). I gently place my hand on Dad's shoulder and shake him. So many emotions are running through my body. *Will Dad be annoyed with me? Will Dad punish me dreadfully? Will I be alive tomorrow?* It doesn't matter – I have to get someone to help me put out the fire. Dad wakes up, and I tell him what is happening. Dad and I go back to my bedroom, with Mum following. Dad gets a sheet off my bed and is able to wrap it around my pillow and, thankfully, in one quick action, throw it out the window. I have no memory of what happened after that or whether I was punished or not.

Year after miserable year, the noise of drunken people yelling and laughing terrified me. One drunken person to deal with was disturbing, let alone a party full of them. My bedroom was on the side of the house where the parties were held. A beautiful big verandah accommodated many parties. The smell of alcohol and cigarette smoke wafting into my bedroom window, along with drunken laughter, was too much to take some nights. I just wanted the noise to stop. On those nights, I never slept. My heart was beating out of control with the anticipation of what would happen if I spoke up.

Anxiety rocked my world, spurring me on to make my agitation heard.

I was around 16 years old, and it was after midnight. I'd had enough and plucked up the courage to tell them what I thought. I opened my bedroom window as far as it would go, lent out and yelled, "Shut up! Shut up! I want to go to sleep. Stop making so much noise. Why don't you all just go home?"

Well, that went down like a lead balloon. I didn't just have Dad yelling abusive expletives at me – other men weighed in and told me where to go. I was in big trouble because I'd embarrassed Dad in front of his friends. Thankfully, I could hear Mum telling Dad not to let me upset him.

"No one cares about her anyway – don't worry about it." Although the comment cut through me, I escaped a bullet that night.

Unfortunately, my dad would get physically abusive with my mum. On more than one occasion, I walked into the kitchen in the morning to find Mum's dressing gown with blood on it. One time, when Dad was drunk, he forced himself on Mum. I could hear what was going on from my bedroom, Mum pleading with Dad to stop as she had her period. She was crying. The noise of her crying was deafening. I was frozen, hiding under my bed covers. I wanted so badly to help my mum, but I couldn't. I felt so useless.

I often wondered why Mum never left Dad. She told me one day that she won't leave her home. The security of having a home of her own was more important to her than her physical safety. Her childhood upbringing, never having a secure home to live in, had impacted her greatly. Nothing was going to make her abandon her home.

We can be our own greatest joy and our own deepest pain.

My unpredictable home life caused me pain no matter the circumstance. I became unpredictable myself – even *I* didn't know what I would do next. Mum, Dad, my sisters and I were in the kitchen one evening. I was around 17 years old. Dad was being his usual, sarcastic self. Throwing awful and hurtful words at me. I was crying. I couldn't take this any longer. *Why does my dad hate me so much? I just want him to love me.* I ran out of the kitchen, wanting to hide forever. I was lying on my bed, sobbing, when my mum came into my bedroom. She said to me, "Don't let him get away with that – you are better than that. Stand up for yourself." She walked out of my bedroom. My mind was racing. Next minute I was standing up beside my bed, and so angry. I marched out to the kitchen.

Dad was leaning against the kitchen bench with a stubby in his hand, his stomach exposed. What I did next has haunted me since that day. I walked up to my dad and told him, "I don't like the way you treat me." I pulled my right arm back and then propelled it forward with as much force and strength as I could muster and punched him square-on in his stomach. He went down like a sack of potatoes. Sliding down the front of the kitchen bench, groaning and holding his stomach until he lay motionless on the floor. I couldn't believe that I just punched my dad. Thoughts raced through my mind. *Have I killed my dad? Will he kill* me *if he isn't dead?* He wasn't dead. But I was starting to wish *I* was. To this day, I do not remember anything that happened after that.

Memory blackouts can be a good or bad thing. Not knowing what happened is sometimes worse than the consequences of remembering.

There was never any peace at home. Looking forward to the Saturday night pictures was my saving grace throughout the week. A happy distraction. All the neighbourhood kids would walk together through the park. Same, but in reverse, after the movies had finished. It wasn't a real theatre – just the town hall decked out with old canvas slingback chairs that sat proudly on the hall floor. There was no such thing as comfortable seating back then. It didn't matter – we were young and healthy. If I had to sit in one of those seats now, it wouldn't be a pretty sight watching me try to get into an upright position.

Movies featuring Elvis Presley and James Bond were shown on reels powered by an electric projector. No digital technology back then. On occasion the movie reel would break. Loud cries of, "Oh no!" "What happened?" "Hurry up and fix it!" were heard from the audience below. While we waited for the movie to be fixed, the noise of Jaffas being rolled down the aisles rang out through the hall. Raucous laughter followed as these Jaffas hit their target. Maybe a piece of rubbish, a handbag sitting harmlessly on the floor or a shoe sticking out into the aisle. Everything was fair game. Happy times.

When my sisters and I got home, there would usually be a table full of drunk people there. And you guessed it – I would be singled out and blamed for whatever Dad could think of. Perhaps he thought we got home too late from the pictures, the paint on the ceiling was peeling, or they had run out of beer. All of it was *my* fault. *I cannot be too happy. I hate my life.*

I was old enough to get my driver's licence but the fear of driving was too great. I eventually pushed past my fear and got my licence. Mum and Dad bought me a second-hand Holden sedan. My independence opened up a whole new world for me. Driving many exciting places, to remove myself from my unpredictable home life, was a blessing. Having to eventually go back home was a curse.

I was still working for my dad when a position came up at the bank in town. I applied and thankfully I got the job. After a couple of years, I was invited to join the bank's relieving staff. *Wow, I can finally get away from here. I will definitely take the job.* I was so proud of myself.

My bubble of happiness was burst when I spoke with my father about leaving.

His response cut right through me: "You are not going anywhere."

I was devastated. *See? See? Don't ever be happy, you idiot.* Unfortunately, I had developed a habit of stopping off at the local store and buying Tim Tam biscuits to eat on the way home. They were comfort food, a chance to feel good before I got home, just in case I walked into a shit storm. I wasn't allowed to eat rubbish before dinner, so it was my little secret. Something that was mine. This habit has followed me all my life. Binge eating crap food is a telltale sign that I have been triggered.

My life at that point was spiralling out of control. I tried so hard to be what my parents wanted. I tried so hard to keep out of the way, stay invisible, so I wouldn't be the focus of their attention, good or bad. My parents' unpredictable behaviour was the devourer of my existence.

Along the way, I met a young man who I thought was cool. He became my boyfriend for a while. He dropped me home one night after the movies. We sat in his car for a little bit, doing what teenagers do. Don't worry – I behaved.

Entering the house, I quietly opened the front door and crept past my parents' bedroom on my way to my bedroom. I was happy and content. Just as I reached my bedroom door, Dad came up behind me. He was still drunk from the Saturday night party they'd had. He frightened the crap out of me. *What have I done wrong now? I haven't even been at home.* The look on Dad's face was menacing.

"You stayed in the car for too long. Take your pants off. I want to see if you had sex."

I was horrified. I didn't know what to do. Dad was coming closer and closer to me, then he started shaking me. I was sure he was going to try and take my slacks and underpants off. Thankfully, Mum came into my room and told Dad to stop. She pulled him away and they both left me alone. My heart was racing, my palms were sweating, I was so bewildered. *What just happened? I don't understand. Why does he treat me like this?*

Like other times when I couldn't sleep, I lay in my bed with my little pillow and the covers over my head, praying that Dad wasn't going to come back into my bedroom. Having a boyfriend could have been a happy and exciting experience for me, but my father ruined that. This experience cemented my beliefs. *It is not safe to be happy. I am not good enough.* Thinking I was going to be seen naked by my father had only added to my depressive episodes.

Life at home was worsening as Dad drank more and more. Mum was void of any emotion or female support for me. My hormones were having their own party, and I wondered if I may venture into the unknown and allow myself to have sex. I know, shock horror. So, I decided to talk to Mum. Holy shit – our conversation was short and sweet.

"Would it be okay if I went on the pill?" Mum answered, "Go ask your father." She didn't even look up from what she was doing. I was horrified. I wanted to throw up. Her answer came without hesitation or thought for my emotional state, especially after she had to step in to help me, not so long ago, that night with my boyfriend and Dad's horrific reaction. I do not remember the conversation I must have had with Dad, but I was allowed to go on the pill. However, Dad wouldn't allow me to fill my prescription in town. Instead, it happened via post. Heaven forbid people knew I was taking the pill.

Dad's standing in the town was more important than me.

Things at home were getting to me and I started drinking. Yes, just like my parents. I went off the rails for a bit, as much as I could in a small country town. One night, I ended up sitting in the gutter – drunk as a skunk – feeling like crap after a farewell party for a work colleague.

It was about one o'clock in the morning and I had to go to work that day. I couldn't give a shit though. I got myself upright and staggered home. *I don't want to go home, but where else can I go?*

I must have made a lot of noise as my mother greeted me.

"I am so sick..."

"Stick your fingers down your neck and make yourself sick. You will be okay then." *She is such a cold bitch. No "I will hold your hair for you", or any sort of love. But hey! I should be used to her unloving detachment by now.* So down my throat my fingers went. I threw up, had a shower and went to work.

CHAPTER 5

Hurt

Mother, Father, Grandfather
Is it abuse, or is it love?
Listen to the words
Soft like a dove
The hurt is done
They have had their fun
Is it learnt?
Can it be overturned?
Do they want to change?
Would it be too strange?
Parent of parents
A product of their descendants
Mother, Father, Grandfather
Could my world be any darker?

—Jo Wilcox

It was New Year's Eve and I was around 19 years old. My parents had gone to my aunt and uncle's house to party. I was allowed to have some friends over at our house. My friends and I were having a great time. Behaving, because I wouldn't dare do otherwise, if I wanted to stay alive.

In a small country town in the early 1970s, no one cared about drinking and driving. I saw Dad pull into the driveway. *He is just coming back for more alcohol.* He headed straight for the beer fridge downstairs, but there wasn't any beer. He stumbled awkwardly up the stairs, onto the verandah where my friends and I were, and started yelling at me. "Where's my bloody beer, you piece of shit! Tell your friends to get the hell out of here."

My friends and I were terrified. I had no idea that someone had been helping themselves to Dad's beer and they had cleaned him out. My friends left me. I don't blame them. Trying to explain anything to a rum-drunk man is like talking to a brick wall.

"Dad, I don't know what you are talking about."

His eyes were bulging out of his head, veins popping out of his neck. The look he gave me was horrifying. He was sweating. His speech was slurred. I was petrified. *Holy shit – he is going to kill me tonight.* I had never seen him so out of control. How he made it home without having an accident was a miracle. Before I knew it, he had grabbed me by my neck and was dragging me through the house towards my bedroom, yelling and verbally abusing me. I was absolutely terrified for my life.

Over the years when I had been frightened by Dad, I would give him this *look*. I would just stare. Keep staring, not blinking. He hated it. Unfortunately, this time, it made Dad so much angrier. By the time we reached my bedroom door, I was being choked by my own father.

He flung me into my bedroom. I landed heavily on the corner of my dressing table. I was in dreadful pain, but I wasn't going to let him know that. I was crying uncontrollably, waiting for him to follow me into my bedroom and kill me. My fear was paralysing. As I lay on the floor, he just looked at me and stumbled away. I was exhausted emotionally, mentally and physically, but so relieved.

I dragged myself off the floor and sat on my bed. Our house backed onto a big park. I could hear my friends talking in the park. I was so embarrassed that my friends had witnessed my father's outrage. My bedroom was on the second floor. I remember thinking: *If it had been on the ground floor, I would have climbed out the window, run away and never come back*. The reality was no, I wouldn't – I was too scared of him. I stayed curled up on my bed for hours, not game enough to go to sleep in case Dad came back. I was still awake in the morning.

All of the times Dad went off his nut at me, I never got an apology. Life just went on.

It is hard to have a life when you are constantly in a state of flux, never knowing what is going to happen next.

I had a parent who was unpredictable. Sober, a loving man. Drunk, a monster. I learnt to keep out of the way. I basically lived in my bedroom. It was my place to create, my place of solitude and peace, situated at the back of the house.

I had quite a small room with a wooden bed built onto the wall, with large storage drawers underneath. A dressing table with a bevelled mirror attached, and small doors hiding my most precious possessions. There was also a wardrobe where I kept my clothes, shoes and other bits and pieces. The most important piece of furniture in that room was my desk. I sat at this desk for hours. I always kept my bedroom door shut as I got older. I was safe in this room. The lyrics of the song *In My Room* by the Beach Boys encapsulate my thoughts and emotions that are connected to the hours every day I spent in my room.

My saving grace was painting. I would paint anything, from a picture the size of a postage stamp, that I found rummaging through old magazines, to a tea towel sized picture that I liked. I spent a long time on these drawings and paintings, meticulously shading with dark and light pencils, and colouring with all the hues of the rainbow. I had several different sized paint brushes, which enabled me to create just the right shape, maybe a swirling effect, or just a straight line, that I needed to finish a painting to my satisfaction. I would enter the local shows, receiving first prizes and occasionally show champion.

It was such a thrill to walk into the show pavilion and see my entries displayed. Information cards were placed strategically at the corner of my art, telling anyone who looked my name, age and what prize I had won. These events were mine to celebrate. As I walked around the show, people I knew would congratulate me.

"Hey, Jo, love your painting."

"Good on you, Jo. Champion of the Show this year! Keep it up."

I was grinning from ear to ear, cherishing the recognition I was getting. Show day was a great day. Even though Mum and Dad were not very demonstrative in showing their support, I hoped they were proud of me and the prizes I won. Growing up, I would rather draw and paint than anything else, but always in the sanctuary of my bedroom.

I married my first husband in 1975. I was 20 years old. My life at home was dreadful. My parents had sold the family home and bought a corner grocery store. We were all living in very cramped accommodation at the back of the store until the new house was built. My father was drinking excessively by then. Living two shops away from the pub was too convenient for a man who had no control over his drinking.

The night before my wedding was a Friday night. Friday night was pub night for my mother and father. I asked Dad to come home early as I needed to get a good night's sleep. My grandma had also arrived for my wedding. Dad came home late, drunk as a skunk. I was woken up. I couldn't take it any longer. My anger and frustration were no longer bubbling just below the surface. That unforgettable night, my emotions exploded. I didn't even try to filter the hurtful words that spewed out of my mouth.

Still seething with rage, I got dressed and left the house. I was so hurt that my father did not think enough of me that he could forgo getting drunk just one Friday night. I walked around town in the dark, crying hysterically. I didn't want to go home but I didn't know where else I could go. Lisa lived a few streets away, so I went to her place. Her car was parked in the driveway, unlocked. I slept on the back seat for a few hours. I knew I had to go home. I was getting married. Neither my mum nor grandma said anything to me when I walked into the house.

The previous night was just swept under the rug, never to be spoken about again.

I was a wreck, riddled with anxiety, but at the same time trying to keep positive, having a happy look on my face when my bridesmaids arrived to get their hair and makeup done with me. I ended up getting some calm-me-down tablets from the chemist to hopefully get me through the day. I didn't tell anyone the real reason I needed to be medicated. "Just nervous about the day" was my excuse.

I didn't see my father until I arrived at the front of the church. I was so angry with him, but I also loved him so much and I wished with all my heart he was different. I walked with my father down the aisle to my soon-to-be husband, who had also been drinking. *I can't believe it.* I had to hold him up while we knelt in front of the altar. *What are you doing? You are going from the frying pan into the fire.*

By the time the reception ended, my husband was too drunk to drive so I drove us to our honeymoon on the Sunshine Coast. Our car had a front bench seat. He was lying asleep with his head on my lap. I had stopped at an intersection, crying my eyes out because I was lost. I knew I had made a big mistake. My new husband was just like my dad. The only difference was that he was a happy drunk. Not that that is right, either. I loved my new husband just like I loved my dad. *Why don't they love me enough to not drink to excess? I am not good enough for them – they need alcohol to put up with me.* Hindsight is a wonderful thing. But we do what we do at the time.

We were only married a few months when I developed a blood clot in my leg. Bed rest for a while and no more contraceptive pill. Of course, with no pill, I was soon pregnant with my first child.

When I found out, I was so excited to tell my parents they were going to be grandparents again. I walked into the shop and asked if I could speak with them privately. That wasn't to be. They kept working. I followed them around the shop like a lost puppy, telling them my happy news. This event was so distressing for me I don't remember what their reaction was, or what they said. I do remember that my feeling of worthlessness overtook my excitement and happiness. I walked away from my parents, sobbing.

My beautiful daughter, Kylie, was born in 1976. I breastfed her and I loved every minute of it. My happy, carefree life with my beautiful daughter was marred by Postpartum Depression (PPD). My doctor prescribed antidepressants. I was hallucinating, unable to sleep and not coping. I told my doctor I could not take the antidepressants. He didn't listen to me. He knew better, telling me to just stick with it for a little longer.

My life was spiralling out of control, leaving me broken and disillusioned. The depression and anxiety I already lived with fed the PPD. I was losing it big time.

Unfortunately, I was on my own. My husband's mother passed away when he was a child, leaving me without a mother-in-law to go to. My mother didn't help me. Having the corner store took up all her time. It was in the too-hard basket to visit her daughter and granddaughter. Out of sight, out of mind.

Before long, the unthinkable happened when I couldn't bear the way I was feeling any longer. One day, Kylie wouldn't stop crying. I am sure she was picking up on my anxiety, fear and sense of worthlessness as a mother. I was so distraught, I tried everything. I fed her, changed her, bathed her, cuddled her, tried to soothe her. Nothing worked. I was crying and overwhelmed by hopelessness. I was standing by her cot, and I dropped her into it. Within a split second, I realised what I had done. *Oh my god! What have I done? Did I hurt my daughter? Is she okay?*

I picked her up and hugged her so close. I was devastated. My guilt was strangling me, I couldn't breathe. I fell to my knees and curled up on the floor next to the cot and cried and cried. Holding her close to my heart, rocking back and forward, trying to soothe both of us. As I settled, so did she. Eventually she fell asleep. I remained lying on the floor, so I didn't wake her up, as she needed to sleep.

This episode taught me something about myself. I know how my body works. I know what I can and cannot take. *I am no longer going to take what a doctor says as gospel. My body, my decision, within reason of course.* I weaned myself off the antidepressants. As the insidious drug left my body, my sanity returned. My daughter was happier and more settled also. I wonder, today, if the antidepressants I took affected Kylie as well, seeing as I was breastfeeding her. I will never know.

That was when my journey with alternative modalities started. I believe in the medical profession but there are certain people, like me, who just cannot tolerate chemical drugs. Today, thankfully, there are a lot more doctors who also embrace the natural approach.

A few short years went by. My marriage was breaking down. The dreaded alcohol was taking my husband away from me and plonking him squarely on a welcoming bar stool. I wanted so badly for my marriage to work. I should have known better. No one can make an alcoholic stop drinking. I decided to try for another child.

My son, Guy, was born in 1979.

Unfortunately, our little family was still second best to the almighty beer bottle.

Living on a dairy farm was a wonderful, carefree place to raise children. Open spaces, animals roaming free, and no close neighbours. It was my father-in-law's farm. My husband helped run the day-to-day operations. It was hard work though. We milked twice a day, every day. It was 24/7, with minimal time off, but I loved it. We had built our own home on the property. I had my two beautiful children, whom I loved with all my heart.

My father-in-law played lawn bowls on the weekends, so it was my husband's sole responsibility to milk the cows in the afternoons his dad was away. But in his mind, weekends were for drinking with his mates, not milking cows and earning a living for his family.

It was milking time one afternoon and my husband wasn't home yet. I was panicking. The herd of around 120 cows had made their way up to the bales, waiting eagerly to be ushered in to be fed and milked. I had milked the cows before, but not on my own. I had a cot in the bales and a safe space for my kids to play. The afternoon was creeping on. *I am going to have to start milking or it won't get done.* So, I gathered up the kids, toys and food and we all walked up to the bales. After about an hour of milking, I saw my husband drive into our garage. I was so relieved. *Thank goodness, he will be here soon.*

He never came up. *What am I to do?* Kylie was around four years old at the time. *I will send her down to the house and get her to tell Daddy to come and help Mummy.* Because the bales were at the top of a hill, I could see clearly every step she made on her way to our house. She never came back. I was overwhelmed with worry. I stopped the milking machines, picked Guy up out of the cot and ran down to the house. There was Kylie lying on the kitchen floor, crying. I was horrified. *Oh my god! What happened? Is she badly hurt?*

I frantically looked around and noticed vomit on the floor. My husband had spewed up when he came in the house. Kylie had run into the house, slipped in the mess and fell. I was livid. My heart was pounding uncontrollably in my chest. My mind was racing. *Where is he? I am going to kill him.* My priority was to make sure Kylie was okay. Thankfully she was, with just a little bump on her head where she had careened into the kitchen cupboard. She was shaken, but very happy to see me and her little brother.

My husband was very drunk, but he had managed to get himself to the bedroom where I found him sprawled across the bed asleep. I tried to wake him up. No chance. I cleaned Kylie up, changed her clothes and we all walked back up to the bales. The cows had to be milked no matter what went on. I started the milking machines back up, put both the kids in the cot with some snacks and toys, and started working.

About half an hour later, my father-in-law came home from bowls. I knew he could see that there were too many cows waiting to be milked for that time of the afternoon. *He is not going to be happy, and I don't blame him.* He changed his clothes and came to the bales. He was extremely disappointed in the situation unfolding in front of him. The kids were happy to see their granddad, and they had lovely hugs. He asked me where his son was. I told him. He was mad with me, saying, "You shouldn't be here, Jo. Go home. This is no place for you to be with the kids on your own."

I knew his anger wasn't really directed at me. The disappointment and anger he felt towards his son must have weighed heavily on his heart. I gathered up the kids and our bits and pieces and we left to walk back home. My emotions were in overload, worrying about my father-in-law. *He is not a young man – he shouldn't have to finish the milking on his own.* My thoughts turned to my own plight. *I cannot keep doing this. Does my husband realise what he did to our daughter? I am so unhappy. What am I to do?*

Our relationship was strained. We no longer slept in the same bedroom. My husband, although a loving and attentive father when he was home and sober, was drinking our money away. Of course, my childhood traumas stopped me from standing up and being confrontational. On occasion I tried to talk to him about his drinking, and he would just walk away, not saying anything.

The elephant was in the room – we just tiptoed around it. Never resolving the issue.

My mental and emotional capacity to deal with his drinking was spent. I just closed down.

We hadn't had sex for a long time. One night he came home from the pub all apologetic and loving. I was suckered in, and a few months later I was pregnant with my third child. I was still breastfeeding my son, who was 11 months old, and I had the Intrauterine Device (IUD) inserted. I was flabbergasted when the doctor told me I was pregnant. *What are the odds? That shouldn't have happened.* My marriage was not in the right shape to welcome another child.

I arrived home from seeing my gynaecologist, who had to remove my IUD. He warned me that by doing this I may miscarry, but if I didn't remove the IUD it could attach itself to the baby. There was no argument – remove it. The next day I started to bleed. My husband had a fishing trip planned. The fishing trip won. I was left to soldier through this emotional time without his help.

Surgery was performed and I was no longer pregnant. Because of the stressful, unhappy atmosphere at home, my recovery was exhausting.

My father-in-law was a wonderful, caring man. I loved him very much. He adored his grandchildren. Our home was just down the hill from his, so the kids and I would walk up to see him often. One day he said to me, "If you need to leave, I understand." He apologised for his son's behaviour. When I finally made my decision, I went and spoke to him, and he gave me his blessing.

When he passed away many years later, Kylie and Guy wanted to go to his funeral. We went and stood away from the crowd that had gathered around the grave site. They were happy to be there to pay their respects to a man who loved them unconditionally. I know in my heart that he would have been smiling down on us that day.

CHAPTER 6

Reveal

Just as the tree sheds its bark
To reveal a renewed tall and strong trunk
The survivor loses her dignity
To become no longer tall and strong
Just as the butterfly sheds its cocoon
To reveal colourful wings of flight
The survivor sinks deeper into quicksand, no longer able to move
Just as the snake sheds its skin
To reveal another youthful body
The survivor ages, never again to know a baby's innocence
To be like the tree, the butterfly and the snake
is to allow the strength of youth,
to propel her forward
upon the colourful wings of dignity and hope

—Jo Wilcox

Leaving the home I had created for my little family was devastating. Because we lived on a dairy farm and it was my husband's place of work, I was the one who had to leave. I packed what I could fit into our car, and my kids – then aged six and three – and I drove away. I felt so guilty and sad that I was taking Kylie and Guy away from their dad. He was always welcome to come and see his kids.

I was riddled with anguish as we left. I have never coped well with the unknown. *Will I be able to raise my kids on my own? Will I be able to find somewhere to live? Will they hate me for taking them away from their father? Will they miss the wonderful cuddles they had with their granddad? Will I be able to find work to support us?* I held it together as best I could for my kids – always the strong and sensible one. A few years earlier, my mother and father had moved away from the little country town to Bribie Island, so that is where I headed.

We stayed with Mum and Dad for a short while until I found somewhere to rent. It wasn't easy being in such close quarters with my parents. Dad was still drinking and Mum was not very supportive. Because of Mum's horrible childhood and the insecurities that manifested for her, she wasn't happy that I left the security of our family home.

"You must go back. Think of your children's security," she demanded.

"I can't live with him anymore. I don't feel loved." There was no way to tell her that just existing under the same roof as my husband made me feel second best. There was nothing I could say that helped Mum support my decision. Not wanting to have anything to do with him, I stopped wearing my wedding rings. Well, that was another bone of contention for her.

"They are worth a lot of money – wear them," she argued.

"I don't want to be married to him anymore, so I am not going to wear them." My answers fell on deaf ears. I couldn't win no matter how hard I tried to explain my reasons. She also told me in no uncertain terms that she would not mind my kids so I could go out.

Because of my mother's attitude to my single parent status, I was concerned about making ends meet financially. I decided I would look for work where I could either take my kids along, or work during the times they were at school. I kept my ear to the ground when I was at school and put up little flyers on the school notice board for ironing or house cleaning jobs. It wasn't long before I had money coming in.

I found somewhere to live on the ocean side of the island. It was the top half of a house, with people living underneath us. Not ideal for me. The constant noise of people so close was distressing. The upside was we could walk to the beach, play in the sand and swim in the ocean.

Living in a small country town and then on the farm, I had grown up used to an environment where everyone knew and looked out for one another. I wasn't prepared for the reality of being so close to so many human beings going about their day without any need to interact. There was no "Hi, how are you going?" I didn't know anyone. I had no allies, no friends.

I had to paddle my own canoe, hoping I wouldn't come across any rapids to throw me off course.

Nights were especially hard for me. After I put the kids to bed, I would watch TV for a little while to try to escape into another world, but it was always drowned out by noises from downstairs, along with those of the other neighbours, whose homes were so close that I could hear them all going about their nighttime routines.

My spider senses were alerted. *Oh my god. What is that?* I jumped up and rushed to the window, my heart beating out of my chest. *Shit – it is a child screaming.* Looking across the park, I could see an adult male holding a child by their clothes and shoving them outside into the dark night. The terrified child, who would have been under 10 years old, was standing on a small landing of a two-storey house. Ear-piercing screams and thunderous banging penetrated my consciousness as the child bashed on the door to be let back in. My own fears took over. I was frozen in time.

I wanted to run away but I couldn't. I understood this scenario too well. Every noise around me was amplified a thousand times. The TV was yelling at me, the fridge motor was vibrating through me as though it was going to break me into tiny pieces, never to be whole again. I was so fearful for that small, petrified child. I was helpless.

I was that little child – their terror was my terror. Stuck in my past, trauma dictated my reaction to what was unfolding in front of me. Beside me was a little table covered in colouring books and many coloured pencils. It had been a scene of happiness earlier in the day, where my kids' imagination helped them to create with boundless abandon. The items on this table now became a source for harm, not happiness.

My head was splitting with pain, my palms were sweating, my heart was racing faster than the speed of sound. My own silence was deafening against the screams of the child. Even in my traumatic state, my thoughts were for the safety and happiness of my own children. I couldn't make a sound; I didn't want to scare my kids. *I want to scream. I want to run at this man and kill him. I want to hide.* So many conflicting actions pulled me in different directions all at the same time.

I understand now what was happening to me. I was reliving the many abuses I had suffered. The overwhelming agony of being thrown back in time opened wounds that were still so close to the surface. My debilitating fear turned into rage. The next thing I remember was seeing blood streaming down my forearm. I had no idea why I was bleeding. I looked around and saw the scissors that my kids had been using covered in blood.

What have I done?

It seemed like hours had passed. Looking at my watch, it had only been a matter of minutes. Minutes I don't remember. Minutes I won't get back. *What is happening to me? Am I having a nervous breakdown?* Dragging myself away from the window, I grabbed some tissues to hold over my wound. In a panic, I thought: *my kids, my kids, are they okay?* I raced to their bedroom, sick with worry. They were sound asleep, hopefully having beautiful dreams.

I came back to the window just in time to see that mongrel of a man pull the sobbing child back inside. I bandaged up my arm and thought up a plausible excuse to tell my kids in the morning. Another day where I have to pretend I am hunky-dory.

My new life brought new challenges for both me and my kids.

A year or so went by, and Guy became sick. Trips to the doctor were numerous, but no one could tell me what was wrong with him. *What am I to do? If the doctors cannot fix him, how am I going to help him?* One day, Guy was sitting on my lap on the lounge. The next minute he was so agitated, he tried to climb out the window behind us. I grabbed him, pulled him away from the window and walked into the middle of the room. He didn't look right. His eyes were glazed, he was making funny noises. I was so scared he was going to die.

I rang the doctor and was instructed to take him to the hospital. My little boy was only around three years old. I contacted my mum, explained the situation and, thankfully, she was eager to help me, coming along with us to the hospital. On arrival, I found the children's ward. It was cold and uninviting, with nurses who were more like prison wardens than loving and caring people. They were to be my son's caregivers.

After some tests were done, I was told I had to leave him at the hospital overnight. I was devastated. "I will stay with him, so he is not upset." *They will be grateful that my son will be easier to attend to with me there*. But that wasn't the procedure back then.

"Go home – you cannot stay here. You are to be back here at 7am. No earlier," I was informed.

Oh my god. Who does she think she is, treating me like that? I am his mother. I need to be with him.

No matter how much I tried to accept what I was just told, the guilt of leaving my little boy in a place he didn't know, with people he didn't know, was eating me alive. I was crying uncontrollably as Mum led me back to the car. When I got back to my parents' house, I was a mess. Dad was so supportive and caring. He hugged me so tightly I thought I was going to break. I was so grateful for the love and support my parents showed me that night. I don't know how I would have coped without their help.

I bathed and fed Kylie and put her to bed after many cuddles and kisses. Needless to say, I didn't sleep at all that night. Being a victim of the unknown was eating me up inside. I was to suffer in silence until 7am the following morning when I could see my son again.

Again, I felt the debilitating pressure of helplessness enter every fibre of my being.

I was up early, had breakfast and drove down to see Guy. I arrived just before 7am. I walked into the ward to find him sobbing. His little body shaking. I could tell he had been crying for a long time.

Another nurse yelled, "Where have you been? Why weren't you here earlier? Your son has been crying all night. You are a useless person." I was devastated, but, with the conviction of a lioness protecting her cub, I let her have it.

"How dare you speak to me like that. I was told by the nurse yesterday I had to go home. I couldn't stay with my son, and I was to be back here at 7am this morning." I paused for a moment and then continued. "Get someone who knows what they are doing to tell me about my son's condition."

I took Guy home that day. The next day, he was sicker than when I took him to the hospital. I found out staff had put my son in the ward with babies who were infected with a very contagious virus, which had been killing them. Back to the doctor we went, and I thanked my lucky stars Guy didn't have to go back into hospital. All I could do was love and care for him. He eventually recovered. No one else got the virus, so it was a positive end to a harrowing experience for all of us.

The pressures of being a single mum were taking their toll. I was still suffering from debilitating migraines. *How do I recover from a migraine when I have two young kids to look after? I cannot just go to bed and leave them unattended.* I would gather up books, the potty, bottles, cups, food, clothes, and their favourite toys and bedding, and the three of us would live in my bedroom until I could lift myself off my bed and venture out into the rest of the house. My self-esteem was at an all-time low. I was suffering, feeling so unloved. *Will I ever be happy?*

We had to move from our seaside home. I didn't know the landlords could turf us out for holidaymakers who would pay holiday letting prices. Bummer. I finally found an affordable place to rent on the calm side of the island. The kids were both at school – they had made some friends and settled in, which was great.

As time went on, I made friends through the school. I was offered house cleaning and ironing work, which I gladly accepted. This worked out well because I could take the kids with me, if I needed to. I also met some ladies who played squash. They invited me to join them. I was very appreciative of their kindness. Mum had mellowed, allowing me to leave the kids with her and Dad so I could participate in this sport. I was very grateful.

I was enjoying my respite from being a single mum. Playing squash was exhilarating. I was pretty good at it too. After a few weeks, my lady friends introduced me to a man they knew. "He is single and likes you," one of them said with a wink. *How wonderful*, I thought. *He likes me*. My track record with relationships wasn't good. I trusted my lady friends and accepted his offer to go out together. We went out a few times and I enjoyed his company. Having someone take notice of me was exciting also.

I was at squash this one evening when I saw my lady friends giggling and pointing at me. Not sure what the issue was, I approached them and asked what was going on. They wouldn't say. My spider senses were twitching. I knew something wasn't right. Another lady who I didn't know very well came over and told me about the man I had been dating.

My world crumbled around me. I was stunned to hear her words. "Do you know he is married? His wife is in hospital having his baby." I stood in front of her, tears rolling down my face. *I would never knowingly go out with a married man. With all the traumas I have suffered throughout my life, why would I put another family through emotional pain? Why did these women do this to me? I cannot trust anyone.* I was broken. I felt betrayed. I now understood why these ladies were sniggering behind my back. Their enjoyment was at my expense.

I tried to put this emotionally draining episode behind me. I stopped playing squash, hoping I would never see those horrible people again, and concentrated on my kids. School runs and play dates. It had been around three weeks since those women made me their scapegoat. I was finally starting to feel that I could cope again.

I was preparing dinner for my two kids when I heard a knock at my door. I had never met the lady standing in front of me as I opened the door.

"I am his wife. I have just had his baby. Why did you do what you did?" My mind was foggy, I couldn't think rationally. The shock of having his wife stand in front of me, accusing me of instigating this scenario, was overwhelming. I had been sucker punched. I couldn't get my breath. I just stood there. All I could say to her was, "I am so sorry."

I must be the most gullible person on the planet. It is not only men I cannot trust, but women too.

Living my life in small country towns did not prepare me for the big wide world. I learnt the hard way that trust can be brutalised. Whether I was a bitch or a kind-hearted person, some humans do not care. The feathering of their nest and the exponential growth of their ego is all that matters.

I wished for a safe place to land while I carried my silent burdens.

The guilt and shame attached to this memory etched deep in my soul the belief that I was worthless, no good and didn't deserve to live. The little self-esteem I had plummeted to lows I hadn't experienced before. I felt dirty and unlovable. A self-destructive cycle began that day, leading me down a path that I couldn't see my way out of.

CHAPTER 7

Unknown shame

"If you put shame in a Petri dish,
it needs three things to grow exponentially:
secrecy, silence and judgement.
If you put the same amount of shame in a Petri dish
and douse it with empathy, it cannot survive."

—Dr Brene Brown

TED Talk: Listening to Shame

"You are a bloody slut!" Dad bellowed, veins popping out of his neck. I looked at him in total disbelief. The familiar feeling of anxiety ripped through my entire body, my palms were sweating, the pounding of my heart hurt in my chest. Fear gripped me like a vice that was being turned ever so slowly, squeezing every inch of life out of me. As tears started rolling down my face, I went back to those familiar questions, asked many times over the years. *What have I done? Slut? Why would my father say this to me?* My already battered state was destroyed beyond reasoning.

I was struck with emotional silence, unable to think, to defend myself, to ask him why he said this. *Why doesn't he realise that I don't know?* I was alone in a darkness I had not experienced before. I was on my own.

I managed to open the back door and stumble outside. Feeling faint, I sat on the back stairs of my parents' home, sobbing. I was destroyed. Hopelessness engulfed me. With every tear that escaped from my downturned eyes and splattered on the step below, a small part of me died. To this day, I cannot remember if my father told me why he called me a slut. I zoned out completely.

I dragged myself off the stairs and gathered up the kids. Trying to get my head straight, we went to the beach, had a swim and made sandcastles together. All the while, I was trying to make sense of what my father had just accused me of. I didn't have any information that would get me closer to an answer. My memory bank was completely blank.

Once back home, the kids had dinner, and I put them to bed with hugs and kisses. *I need a drink.* I sat up drinking, trying desperately to forget the day. Not being able to sit upright anymore, I crawled into bed, hoping the next morning I would wake up and my abusive life would all be a dream.

Again, I felt the debilitating pressure of helplessness enter every fibre of my being.

The turmoil of the past 30-odd years had finally broken me. Grief from losing so much during my life was my punishment, and alcohol became my escape from reality. I was so screwed up mentally and emotionally that I was driven to the edge of insanity.

A few days went past, and I asked myself: *how could my life get any worse?* The kids were in bed. I watched TV for a bit, no alcohol that night, I was too hungover from the nights before. I was so tired and depressed. I took myself off to bed, took some migraine tablets and finally drifted off into a deep sleep. My dreamtime was disturbed by what I thought was a knock at my front door. I froze in fear. *Surely it isn't that lady coming back to berate me some more over her husband.*

I gingerly got out of bed, threw on my dressing gown and crept silently to the lounge room. There was no way I was going to open my door unless I knew who was there. It was after midnight. I was able to pull the curtain back enough to peer out the window without being noticed. There was a man standing there... a man I had never seen before. My body shook and I tried to make sense of why he would be at my door.

"Jo, let me in, let's have some fun," he yelled, slurring his words while gripping the door handle to hold himself steady. O*h my god. How does he know my name? What fun does he want to have*? My gut was doing flip flops, alarms and bells were going off in my head. *Danger! Danger!*

I stayed really quiet, peering through the slightly parted curtain, waiting anxiously for him to leave. I watched as he went down the stairs, stumbled to his car and drove away. My head was swimming. I didn't understand what had just happened. *Why can't I remember him? What have I done? Have I been that drunk I don't remember?*

After this frightening ordeal, my drinking escalated to a level of concern. I was stuck in an uncontrollable landslide of guilt, shame, self-hatred and utter hopelessness. I was losing it big time. The wheels had fallen off my already wobbly wagon.

I woke one morning in agony. My memories of horror had manifested physically in my body. I ached all over. Everything that happened that day irritated me. I was in pain, I was anxious, I was depressed, and I hated myself. The kids picked up on my emotional state and were also out of control. I couldn't take the noise of them fighting anymore.

I was so angry. I felt trapped. I had to get away. I sat them both on the lounge.

"Sit here, don't you move. I am leaving, I cannot take your fighting anymore. I will be back. Don't you move off this lounge."

I went downstairs, got on my push bike and rode away. Luckily, I didn't drive my car because by that stage I was sobbing uncontrollably. I could see no way out of this mess. I was being buried under more and more things that were out of my control. I was trapped in a body riddled with soul-destroying memories I was unable to deal with.

I do not remember how long I was away from my children. I hope with all my heart it wasn't long. I rode around, crying hysterically, wishing I could end my life. *Wanting* to end my life. I finally came back to the house, walked upstairs and saw my beautiful little kids were still sitting on the lounge, crying. *What have I done? I am my mother and father. I am doing to my precious kids what my parents did to me. I am useless. I don't deserve to be the mother of these amazing little beings.* I hated myself.

I grabbed both my kids and hugged them. "I'm so sorry. I was wrong. It's not your fault. I will never leave you again."

I was more worried about staying with my innocent children. *What if I hurt them? What if I have a complete breakdown in front of them? What if they saw me self-harm?* My actions that day have haunted me every day since. The shame I cling to makes sure I do not forget when I was so emotionally destroyed that I chose to leave my children on their own.

I asked my kids about this incident when they were adults. Guy told me he didn't remember it. Kylie's reaction was a different matter completely. She didn't say too much. The look she gave me was enough. My daughter turned to me with disbelief and said, "But you left us."

I was destroyed knowing that my unbelievable actions on that dreadful day had also haunted my beautiful daughter all these years. All I could do was apologise. Nothing else I could have said or done would have helped her deal with the emotional suffering I caused.

The 1980s for me were horrendous. Everything that could go wrong did go wrong. My drinking continued, causing me not only emotional and mental deterioration but also hindering my finances. I was a wreck, but I tried really hard to keep it together for my kids. Of course, I would never let on to my parents that I was struggling. What went on behind closed doors stayed behind closed doors. Just like how I dealt with my step-grandfather's abuse.

I was responsible for two beautiful children. Their welfare was paramount to them growing up to be happy, heathy and well-adjusted people.

Consciously, this was my ultimate goal – to give my kids the childhood I never had.

Unconditional love from me, time to play and explore their worlds, and the hope that they would grow up loving me, not despising me like I despised my parents. But my hurts and the fallout from being abused so young had left me floundering in a sea of agony and unimaginable self-loathing. Having let my children down and being a source of pain for them was the biggest shame I had to come to terms with.

During a routine doctor's appointment, it was revealed I had an abnormal Pap smear. My gynaecologist performed a procedure, while my kids stayed with my parents.

Having this happen was a double whammy for me. I had been working part-time at the pre-school before applying for a full-time position. The extra money would have been so helpful because of my financial problems. I remember sitting across from the pre-school director, who knew about my health problem. She said, "We cannot take the risk of giving you the full-time position, as it may be a while before you are well again."

I still kept my part-time teacher aid job. I was also the crossing guard (lollipop lady) and school cleaner. I still did house cleaning and ironing. All part-time or casual jobs, so having to take time off was not good because I didn't have access to any holiday or sick pay. I managed to struggle through.

After the surgery, I had regular Pap smears to make sure the pre-cancer cells were all gone. I was so grateful that after a couple of years of clear results, I was told I was free of the pre-cancer cells. Woohoo.

I was in my late twenties, early thirties in the 1980s. I'd had two births, one miscarriage, my tubes tied, and a procedure for cervical pre-cancer cells – all overseen by my gynaecologist. Throughout these appointments, I allowed him to take advantage of me. My history of sexual and verbal abuse only cemented my belief that I wasn't worthy – that no one would ever love me.

You may ask, "Why didn't I change gynaecologists?" That is a good question. I do not remember ever thinking of that as a solution.

I look back at what he did, and I am gripped by immense shame and guilt. *Why didn't I tell him to stop? Why didn't I report him? Why? Why? Why?* I will never know the answers to these questions. I was again at the mercy of a man whose self-gratification came before my healing.

As a child enduring sexual abuse from my step-grandfather, I was too young to help myself, to push him away, to tell someone, to scream. As an adult, I chose to succumb. More shame manifested from this act of cowardice.

I remember a specific incident. The gyno welcomed me into his consultation room. I sat across from him at his desk; we chatted and then he took me into the procedure room. The familiar sterile bed rested unceremoniously against the wall, with the foot of the bed in full view of his desk. The room wasn't very big – I always felt trapped in this cramped space. A small chair waited to catch my clothes as they were discarded. He always accompanied me into this room. He always watched me undress and get up on the bed.

During this visit, he produced a vibrator. I was very upset, but I tried really hard not to show it. He wanted to see if the vibrator would help me to achieve an orgasm. I had never seen a vibrator before, so it took me a bit to realise what he had in store for me. I wanted to run out of the room. Instead of being in fight or flight mode, I found myself in fawn. Not wanting him to hurt me, I went into people-pleaser mode, compliant in every way.

At a doctor's surgery, I would normally have a sheet covering my lower body. Not here. I was never covered. I laid there naked, vulnerable and frightened, allowing him to use the vibrator on me. He then wanted me to try. He handed me the device and proceeded to walk to his desk and sit on his chair. As I tried to manipulate the device, with my bare vagina facing him, I thought: *shit – is he playing with himself?*

Horrible memories of my step-grandfather flooded my mind. My heart was racing, but not from having an orgasm – from sheer panic. I stepped down off the bed, with him watching every awkward movement I made. I managed to get dressed, even though my hands were shaking. As I was getting ready to leave the room, he grabbed my hand and placed it on his erect penis. He said to me, "It is okay – I will help you." *Did he think that his behaviour was going to help me like sex? To orgasm?*

At the time, I had no idea the sexual abuse I had suffered as a child was the biggest cause of my sexual distress in adulthood.

My crying during sex because of my inability to orgasm, to allow myself to receive pleasure not only from my partner but from myself, would lead to more uncontrollable crying while I lay curled up in a ball, hiding under the bed covers, wishing I was invisible. My self-loathing tortured me to the point of realising I was unlovable and an immense failure.

I had told the gynaecologist about my dad's dreadful treatment of Mum and the alcoholism I endured while growing up. I thought these were the reasons I was so screwed up sexually, but they were only offshoots of a much darker menace eating away at my consciousness.

Would he have acted differently if I had told him the real reason why I was broken? Who knows.

I felt so dirty, scared and overwhelmed by shame and guilt. It was hard for me to keep my composure long enough to leave his office. As I left, he always gave me a hug and told me, "You have a beautiful vagina." I don't know if he was trying to make me feel good or show that he thought I was a lovely person. I truly don't know. I *do* know that I will never forget those words.

I finally got back to my parked car. I was crying and shaking as I struggled to get the door open. Sitting in my car, I started to scream. *Why do I allow men to abuse me? Why am I so weak? I am a useless piece of shit. Not worth breath. I should be dead. Will my life be forever tainted by the beck and call of the male libido?*

By the time I picked my kids up from school, I was composed enough to greet them with a big smile, kiss and cuddle. Home, afternoon tea, homework, bath, dinner, a story and bed was our routine. It was a Friday. I was grateful there was no school the next day. I tucked the kids into bed with more kisses and cuddles and switched off the light.

As I was walking to the kitchen, a wave of anxiety overwhelmed me. I was shaking, my heart pounding and missing a beat at the same time. My legs felt like jelly. I poured a drink, grabbed both the glass and bottle, and quickly walked to the lounge room. I sat in my recliner, extending the footrest. I wasn't sure if I was having a panic attack or a heart attack. I sculled my glass of Scotch and dry, hoping to drown out these scary feelings.

The aftermath of my gynaecologist appointment was raising its ugly head, shoving me into an episode unlike anything I had ever experienced before. The intensity of emotions that were running through my body kept me unable to move without experiencing horrendous pain. My head was pounding. My body was throbbing with every beat of my heart. I kept pouring myself drinks. *I don't want to feel.* I wanted numbness to overtake my broken body. A couple of hours passed and I was crying uncontrollably.

Every emotion I had stored over the years, every emotion I never allowed myself to feel, was oozing out of every cell of my body.

I was confused. Flashes of past horrendous memories brought more tears, more hopelessness and shame. I was falling apart. I was crying, drunk. I was watching a movie of my complicated and painful life move across in front of my eyes. It was a horror film, starring a vulnerable little girl, a frightened teenager and a cowardly adult.

The impact of all these scenes made me realise that I didn't want to live anymore. My pain was excruciating. My fear was insurmountable. *I am no good to my kids like this. They will be better off without me. I have no more to give.*

I fell out of my chair, grabbing furniture to pull myself up. I stumbled to my bedroom to get my pills. I had been prescribed sleeping tablets, which I hadn't taken yet. I could hardly see the packet, let alone push the bloody tablets out. I eventually managed to rescue all the tablets from their foil prison. My water bottle was on my bedside table, a lucky break. I swallowed all the pills with the water and lay on my bed, thinking I would finally be rid of my pain. I passed out. I am not sure how much time went by before I was violently ill. Throwing up all over myself, my bed and the floor.

I had just experienced my first suicide attempt. Afterwards, when I had my first coherent thought, it was: *I cannot even kill myself.*

CHAPTER 8

Emotions – to feel alive

But to feel alive is not always a positive emotion.
To be alive means to feel both the positive and negative.
A trauma survivor supports the concept of wishing for numbness.
The positive concept of numbness supports the body's heaviness
and allows the mind to stagnate in time.
This, of course, is not ideal.
The wellbeing of someone who has survived trauma is to allow the
emotional, mental, physical and spiritual bodies
to welcome whatever emotion arises.
Bringing with that emotion hope, compassion for
self, and the ongoing awareness that:
To Be Alive Is To Feel.

—Jo Wilcox

It was a dreadful night. I had to clean everything up before the kids got up in the morning. I got no sleep. My head was pounding. The mix of alcohol and too many pills gave me a hangover from hell. I suppose I can thank my oversensitive system for saving my life that night.

Shame is a killer force. Leaving its prey with limited skills to navigate a world that wishes to put down, destroy and immobilise its strongest residents. Shame has entered my life on many occasions.

Will I continue to have shame predict how I respond to my lived embarrassing or humiliating situations?

Will my perception that I have done something immoral or improper continue to leave me with the crippling assumption and unrealistic self-criticism that I am bad?

Or will I employ the positive and be empathetic, nurturing little Jo, showing her the love and acceptance she ached for as she grew into a teenager and then an adult?

Time will tell, I suppose.

After my failed suicide attempt, I worked really hard at reducing my alcohol intake. If I had kept drinking, I would have ended up just like my parents. I truly didn't want that. I didn't want the generational cycle to repeat itself. A few years passed and my kids were enjoying school. I still had my casual and part-time jobs.

It was the late 1980s, early 90s when my life finally started to settle down. My financial position was much better as my alcohol consumption was almost nil. My only worry was accommodation. With the support of my sister, Lisa, I decided to move back to my hometown – something I thought I would never do because it held too many horrible memories.

I lived a couple of doors from a small country church. Hanging out my washing on the rotary clothesline in the backyard, I saw a young lady whom I waved to. I bumped into her while shopping one day and we introduced ourselves. She invited the kids and me to attend Sunday school and the church service.

I wasn't a religious person, though I attended Sunday school as a kid, dressed in my beautiful dresses and pretty hats. I was always very wary because I didn't like the minister – he scared me. I was also very wary of this lady's intention after my previous encounter with women I thought were my friends. *She is the pastor's wife – she must be trustworthy.* The kids and I accepted her invitation, we made new friends and I enjoyed their peaceful, happy energy.

A few months passed, and I was asked if the pastor and his wife could come to my house for a visit in the evening after the kids went to bed. I felt honoured that these lovely people would want to be a part of my life. A date was chosen and I waited eagerly for them to arrive, with biscuits and a cuppa at the ready. We sat and chatted while we enjoyed our refreshments. They wanted to have a look around my home. I found that a little strange, but I complied. I had a small collection of CDs – Fleetwood Mac, The Beatles, The Beach Boys and a few others.

When they noticed my CDs, their demeanour changed from friendly too scary as they proceeded to tell me my music was "blasphemous". They yanked the CDs forcibly off my shelf, chanting, "They are the devil's work."

My heart sank. Within seconds, I was transported from a happy place to my all-too-familiar place of fawning.

Not wanting anyone to hurt me or my kids, I allowed these horrible people to search my bookshelves as well. I was told that my book selection was also inappropriate. I had many books on crystals, essential oils, spiritual teachings, healings and meditations – I suppose in their eyes these were the devil's work too. They confiscated my hard-earned personal belongings. They were ordinary, everyday objects that brought me joy, but in their eyes my meagre possessions were against everything Godly.

Kylie and Guy were sound asleep in their beds when these lunatics approached their bedroom. I was so scared. I didn't want them to hurt my children. They proceeded to chant and pray over my kids, but not lovely, healing prayers. They were performing an exorcism – they kept saying over and over that my kids were possessed by the devil. *These people are insane!* I wanted them to leave. My fear suddenly turned to frightening rage. I pushed these two hypocrites forcefully away from my kids' bedroom.

"If you ever come anywhere near my kids again, I will hurt you. Get out of my house!"

Thankfully, my kids never woke up during this ordeal. Over the years, this memory has popped into my awareness. It is hard for me to understand what these people's end game was. Did they think I was going to be a subservient parishioner, willing to give my money and soul to their church? Or were they just nuts? I will never know. It wasn't ideal living so close to these people. I was pleased to hear later that they were no longer in town.

Time marched on. I wasn't drinking at home anymore. If I went out with friends I might have a drink, but not always. I loved my job at the kindy, and my kids were well and happy. Life wasn't too bad.

I still hadn't told any professionals about my younger years. It was my secret to keep until I felt I could trust enough to bring people into my confidence. Trust had always been an uneasy subject for me. Too many past hurts that spanned all aspects of my life kept me closeted. I would often wonder what I had done that was so horribly wrong to have people think they could treat me with such blatant disregard.

Does it all just come from my childhood traumas, not receiving nurturing from those who were supposed to be my care givers? Is it a karmic thing? Have I re-incarnated this time around to experience as much upheaval and pain as possible?

Am I so used to being abused that I need the abuse to stay in my life, so I feel normal? Do I have "Abuse me" tattooed across my forehead, giving those whose egos thrive on the control and abuse of others a clear path to my door?

Living so close to my sister, it became common for Lisa to drop her kids, Andrew and Katherine, off for a play date while she ran some errands. On one occasion, the four kids were running around happily, enjoying each other's company. I had just made lunch for us all. The kids were sitting at their play table, eating and drinking merrily. I was sitting in the lounge room, enjoying a cuppa, when there was a knock at my door.

The home I was renting was a high-set wooden house supported by stumps. The underneath area was open to the street. The front stairs attached directly to the house – there was no landing. Only part of the yard was fenced.

Opening the front door, I was confronted by a man who I had known since I was a child – a friend and drinking buddy of my father. I hated this man. He scared me as a child, and he still scared me as an adult.

My wary eyes darted around, surveying my surroundings, registering escape routes and safe places to hide.

I knew I had to close the door on this man. My gut was alerting me to danger. I was about to slam the door shut when four happy, smiling, curious kids were all around me. My window of opportunity had passed. I was now forced to keep my cool, so the kids would not be scared.

He was looking at me with glazed eyes. He was drunk and was trying to offer me a box of fruit and vegetables. He was standing on the top step and I tried to decline his offer politely and shut the door. He proceeded to shove the box at me. I had to grab it. My heart was pounding. This man was evil. The hairs stood up on the back of my neck. The kids were playing around me, gently pushing each other, which in turn made me wobble towards him. Holding the box of groceries, I had no free hands to defend myself. All I could think of was to stay calm, so the kids were oblivious to my panic.

My instincts were spot on. While the kids enjoyed their play around me, this despicable man rubbed his hands all over my breasts, stopping to grab my nipples through my blouse. I was sick with fear. All I could do was stand firm and in a position that shielded the kids from what this man was doing. Every sense I had was in overload. I could have pushed this miserable creep down the stairs but then I would be in trouble and the kids would be frightened. I stood my ground, trying not to let my vivid memories unhinge me.

A memory of me sidling up to my step-grandfather, when he wanted one of my sisters to sit on his lap, flashed in front of me. I was putting myself in harm's way to protect my sisters. I was now protecting the little ones I loved dearly from this monster who had invaded our precious time together.

His rough, dirty hands continued to invade my space. His drunken breath assaulted my nostrils. I couldn't breathe – I forgot how to. I never made a sound. I never spoke to the kids. I was numb, paralysed in time. *I want him to stop. Why won't he stop? Please, please, please leave.*

I could see that he was getting wobbly. He only had a step width of board to stand on. Because his hands were all over my breasts, he wasn't holding on to the railings. He finally removed his hands, held on to the railing, turned around and slowly made his way down the stairs.

As soon as I could, I slammed the door shut. Putting a smiling mask on my face, I turned to the kids excitedly and said, "Look! We have some yummy fruit and veggies, isn't that nice?" I was so grateful that none of the kids asked any questions.

I placed the box on the kitchen bench and walked calmly to the toilet, saying to the kids as I went, "Go and see if you can find some flat rocks. We can paint them this afternoon." Down the stairs they skipped. Reaching the toilet my nerves were shattered, my stomach was churning uncontrollably, I was crying silently so the kids couldn't hear, and then I vomited until there was nothing left in my stomach. I immediately started looking for somewhere else to live.

Things were ramping up. I acquired another part-time job with a local newspaper, writing small articles and selling advertising. I was happy with my lot. The kids had started swimming training before and after school. We were all kept very busy.

At that time, living in a small country town meant there weren't a lot of sporting activities for kids to participate in. Guy loved football. As there wasn't any club in town, I decided I would start a junior rugby league club. Mountains of paperwork had to be submitted to the regional head office. When the season started, I was delighted to have many boys sign up to play against our neighbouring clubs. Happy days.

Selling advertising to businesses wasn't easy. A lot of ringing around, pounding the pavement, in one door, out another, always with a big, happy smile on my face. One day, I entered a business to find the owner sitting at an office desk. There was something about this man that I liked. He was cheerful and welcoming.

Each week, I visited his business to collect his advertisement for the next issue of the newspaper. We got to know each other through these visits. I learnt he had three adult sons, he was divorced from his first wife, and he owned his business and a grazing property. He learnt I was also divorced and had two much younger kids. We started seeing each other on a regular basis. I invited him to dinner one night to meet my children. Kylie and Guy liked him too, so that was a positive. He was welcomed into our little family. I always felt I was safe with him and so did my kids.

The local police sergeant was looking for their first ever administration assistant. It was a full-time position. My new male friend suggested I apply for the job. Congrats to me – I got the job. I was over the moon. Happy as a pig in mud. As well as being a police station, it was also the Department of Transport, issuing learner driver tests and renewing driver's licences.

I was still having a lot of trouble with my hormones. I couldn't seem to break out of my depressive state. My periods were dreadfully painful and having to deal with Premenstrual Syndrome (PMS) was debilitating. I had depression, irritability, mood swings and insomnia.

My doctor recommended I see a gynaecologist, a new one, to see if there was anything they could do for me. After a lot of poking, prodding, all sorts of tests and scans, it was suggested that having a hysterectomy may stop the depression. There were no other physical problems.

I was only in my thirties and it was a big decision. *Do I want to have any more kids? Will having the hysterectomy help my depressive state? I definitely don't want any more kids. I will try just about anything to help my depression.*

My decision was yes. I was living on my own with my kids, so I organised a young lady to come and stay with them while I was in hospital. Lisa would look in on them also. The operation went well. I have a scar from one side of my abdomen to the other because it wasn't keyhole surgery like today, so I had a lengthy recovery period.

After a couple of years with a full-time job, I was able to build my own home. *Is my life finally turning around?* The kids and I moved into our new place – a wooden, two-storey, three-bedroom home. A memory of asking Guy to mow the lawn while I was out getting groceries makes me smile. I arrived home to find he had mowed his name into the grass. Standing at the top of the stairs, I could see what an awesome job he did. He was running around being silly and we were both laughing. *Isn't it great to have happy memories wash over you?*

The kids were in high school and they were winning many swimming trophies. The swimming squad would travel to many different cities and towns for swimming carnivals.

Unfortunately, the hysterectomy made no difference to my depression. How I had been feeling for years had nothing to do with my physical body, my counsellor told me years later. It was all fallout from my recurring mental health issues. My step-grandfather's actions so many years ago made it impossible for me to regulate my bodily symptoms. My mind, body and soul were all disconnected.

Triggers were still part of my everyday life. Loud noises and smells were the worst culprits. Sudden noises were the worst.

The unknown for me, in any aspect of my life, is my kryptonite.

Having my children around me was healing. I had always immersed myself in their lives. School, sports and social outings brought me a lot of happiness. At the end of 1993 Kylie had finished Year Twelve and Guy Year Nine. I was approached by a boarding school in Brisbane while we were at a swimming carnival. They wanted Guy to swim for them. This was a fabulous opportunity for him.

So, in 1994 both Kylie and Guy left me for Brisbane. I was devastated. I was prepared for Kylie to leave as she had finished high school and was going to follow her dreams in Brisbane. I was not prepared for Guy to be gone in the same year. He would finish his secondary schooling in Brisbane.

My male friend and I were married in 1994, but I wasn't prepared for how my wedding day would unfold. Some of my soon-to-be husband's sons were not happy about me marrying their father. I was not sure of the reason for their unhappiness. *Was I too young?* There was a 12-year difference between us. *Did they hate that I had children?* It made me very sad that these grown men were so negative about their father's happiness. We knew that having a wedding with both families present would not make for a happy event. A decision was made to keep our wedding secret – from everyone.

My first wedding, including the day itself and the night before, was one of the most painful times in my life. Not having what I truly desired for my second wedding was devastating. I lost focus of my happiness and went along with what my husband-to-be wanted. He didn't want his sons there because they disliked me – hence the secret nature of it. But that meant *my* children weren't to be there either. *I can't get married without my children with me!*

It was also decided that we would be married by a celebrant who lived near my parents, which meant no proper reception, no wedding dress. *Oh my god. I have done it again. I have become the people pleaser. I am so good at it. I would get straight As if people pleasing was a subject.*

I woke up the morning of my wedding with a bloodshot eye. The stress and anxiety, and being triggered by previous trauma responses, had overwhelmed me. *That will look good in my wedding photos.* One of the only conventional things we did was hire a professional photographer. I wore an ordinary dress out of my wardrobe. The witnesses to my marriage, and the only ones there, were three people who caused immense unhappiness and anxiety in my life: my mother, father and grandmother.

At the time, I did not realise how the hurts of my first wedding impacted so dramatically on my second. What I do know is that if I hadn't suffered all the abuses and traumas in my younger life, I may have been in a much better place emotionally, allowing me to embrace both families with love and celebrate the day happily.

Making decisions from a place of love and happiness allows the recipient to bask in memories of blissful awareness of self. Decisions made from a place of trauma objectify the recipient, limiting their growth and overall wellbeing. Their ability to love and to be loved is drastically diminished until another person's pleasure becomes their reality.

CHAPTER 9

Believe

To believe you are anything but love
Is to deny yourself happiness
To believe you are anything but light
Is to deny yourself growth
Open your heart to the wonder that is you
Believe you are enough

—Jo Wilcox

Living in the country, you are at the mercy of the weather. Droughts cause havoc for business and property owners alike. If farmers cannot grow and sell their crops because of the lack of water, searing temperatures or frosts, they cannot support themselves financially. My husband and I fell victim to a drought that gripped Queensland in the 1990s. His businesses and properties suffered, leaving his bank manager no choice but to speak with him about reducing his overdraft. Hard decisions had to be made.

Unfortunately, the drought intensified over the next few years. Plans were put in place to sell up. Stress and depression became a third wheel in my married life. My husband's financial position had worsened dramatically.

The drought's tentacles spread far and wide. Not only did we have to sell everything my husband owned before I met him, my home had to be sold too, as well as our retirement block of land on the Sunshine Coast.

Thank goodness my kids no longer lived with me. It was a great relief knowing that they were stable and secure living in Brisbane. The debilitating mental anguish of not knowing what to do next was excruciating.

Knowing what I know now, I would have been suffering from CPTSD, which also explained the grossly inflated fight, flight, freeze and fawn adrenaline that was coursing through my body 24/7. I had constant migraines, leaving me incapacitated a few days out of the month. I also started drinking again. My world was unravelling. *I don't know how to fix business stuff. I have never owned a business. How do I organise stuff to sell?*

With everything up for sale, my husband and I moved to the Sunshine Coast, his old stomping ground. This also meant that I had to resign from my job with the police service. I'd held this job for seven years. It was very emotional for me because I knew I could have stayed for many more years if my circumstances were different.

In 1996, I was again trying to find somewhere affordable to rent. We both needed an income. Luckily, we found employment quickly.

A pattern was emerging for me. I was happy being married to my husband, thinking I had finally found my happy place, only to be flung into financial ruin. I was so happy having my beautiful, loving children with me, and then they both left. I was happy working for the police service and then I had to leave. I was so happy having my own home to share with Kylie and Guy, and then I had to sell it. My sense of loss was all-encompassing, opening up wounds that manifested from the loss of my innocence as a little one.

My sense of reality was malfunctioning, causing me to travel back in time, to when it was not safe to be happy.

Do I self-sabotage each time my life is progressing positively? Do I subconsciously seek out turmoil and negativity because that has been my normal? I constantly asked myself these questions.

I had heard about an organisation called Al-Anon, which helped families of alcoholics. *Maybe attending a meeting will help me understand my reactions to life.* I pushed through my anxiety and attended a number of meetings – the people were so supportive. It wasn't easy to unburden myself of my experiences with my parents.

This was the first time I had ever experienced any sort of talk therapy. It was definitely an adrenaline rush sitting in these meetings, but not in a good way. Trying to sit still, not fidget, zone out or leave was incredibly difficult. Other people's stories touched my heart, prompting me to remember how unhappy and frightened I was growing up. I found it very confronting and repetitive.

I didn't deal very well with baring my soul on a weekly basis. Days before each meeting, I had anxiety attacks that led to headaches. I was resigned to the fact that I wasn't ready to heal from my past hurts yet. Letting go and moving on is not that simple, especially when you are not emotionally ready. After a few months, I stopped going, knowing that I would have to deal with my history on my own for a little while longer.

My husband and I were travelling back to the country each month to mow lawns, tidy up, and have all the properties in tip top condition for inspections and hopefully a quick sale. Months went by, yet no sales had eventuated. The bank wasn't receiving any payments – things weren't going well. We decided to rent the properties out, so at least some income might appease the bank until we could find a buyer. Our personal finances were horrendous. Rents on the coast were dreadfully expensive compared to the country. We were living off credit cards.

All the properties eventually rented, but we had received demand letters from the bank and I was beside myself with worry. Thinking outside the square, I decided I would travel to Brisbane and get as many telephone books as possible for areas I hoped would be interested in our properties. I came home and started faxing real estate offices. It was immensely time-consuming and laborious, but it gave me a sense of purpose.

My drinking had escalated again. With every drink, I felt the pain that lived in every cell of my body became more bearable.

My fragile coping mechanism chugged along like a little wind-up toy, waiting for a playful child to come along and turn the key to restore its balance.

I had difficulty concentrating, and my emotional outbursts put my husband and me on a destructive path.

Nightmares invaded my nights, leaving me with disturbed sleep patterns. During my waking hours, hopelessness and suicidal thoughts shattered my already fragile ego, leading me to believe everything that was happening was my fault.

By late 1997, the stress and financial burden of moving only added more pressure to our predicament. I had to get away, relax for a bit. I travelled to Hervey Bay, having a few days of me time. Of course, nothing stopped. I still received phone calls from real estate offices and banks. Life just went on, no matter where I was.

My husband had washed his hands of everything. I am sure he was depressed and extremely worried about our future. I became the sole contact for all things financial. Every waking moment, I was fielding phone calls, answering emails and trying to keep our financial boat afloat.

You would think that being on holiday would be a welcome change. Unfortunately, it only gave me the privacy to allow the anger I had been suppressing for years to explode. I was able to drink without anyone telling me I'd had enough. The guilt of making the wrong decision again – trusting another man – was taking its toll.

I could end it all now – no one would know. No one bloody well cares about me anyway. These thoughts rattled around in my head for hours until I couldn't take it anymore. *I cannot leave a mark. This is our little secret – you mustn't tell anyone.* I was drunk, and my step-grandfather's words were taunting me. Looking around, I spotted my nail file on the table. *That will work.* Without hesitation, I started stabbing my stomach. Through my drunken haze, I noticed blood oozing through my blouse. I fell asleep in the lounge chair, waking up hours later to find my wounds had stopped bleeding. *I couldn't care less that I have small holes in my body. No one will see them.*

As the saying goes, "I am not the mistakes that I have made".

Trying to gather the strength to keep putting one foot in front of the other before I got back home was incredibly hard when I didn't believe I deserved success, kindness or love.

More than two years had passed since we put everything on the market and renting the properties out was becoming a nightmare. Bad tenants had left the properties dirty, with rubbish everywhere and unkempt lawns. We couldn't afford to pay someone to clean up, so we were constantly travelling back to clean. I couldn't see a way out of this mess. At least a couple of properties had sold, but we were far from in the clear.

If I wasn't stretched enough, my parents had informed me that my grandmother was going to move to Queensland to live. *Why? Mum, Dad and Grandma hate each other.* I knew living close would be disastrous. A few days later, Mum's aunty, who lived near Grandma, passed away. I was asked if I would drive my parents down to New South Wales for the funeral and, while we were there, we would sort out Grandma's stuff in preparation for her trip to Queensland.

What am I to do? The thought of being trapped in a car with my parents for 10 hours was excruciating. I relented and agreed to take them. The bank was becoming too much for me to handle. Constant phone calls and more demand letters overwhelmed me. This was the icing on the cake. *How am I going to cope?*

We were having a good trip and traffic was bearable, but the closer we got to our destination, the more agitated Mum got. She became angry, saying she didn't want Grandma to come to Queensland to live. I don't blame her. Grandma treated her horribly growing up. She didn't have any filters – she was blunt, cruel and sarcastic. Many times, she upset and belittled members of my extended family, bringing them to tears. She never thought Dad was good enough for Mum, so Dad wasn't her favourite person.

When Grandma come to visit, she wouldn't stay with my parents – she stayed with me. Always me. I was always the one who had to try and fix a person or situation. I had these situations thrust upon me, never with any regard for my feelings or what I may be going through at the time.

We arrived safely. My phone never stopped ringing, but I ignored everything. *It can wait until tomorrow.* After the funeral, Mum, Dad and Grandma decided they would go to the bowls club for drinks. I wasn't invited. I mentioned to Dad that I was asked to go to dinner at my aunty Wilma's home. She is Mum's cousin. Aunty Wilma and I have always been close. We talk on the phone regularly. Her wisdom and support have been invaluable to me as I navigate my unpredictable life. I love her dearly.

"You cannot go. You have too much to do here – you have to clean Grandma's house," Dad barked before he went off to get drunk. I was in my forties and my miserable father was still controlling me.

You may ask, "Why didn't you stand up to him? You were an adult." It wasn't that easy. My self-esteem was at an all-time low, and my financial situation was causing unimaginable stress, agitation and fear. I was grieving all the losses I had endured in my life. My bucket was empty and I couldn't handle any confrontation. Giving in was the best I could do. Grandma's house had two bedrooms. My bed was the lounge, so I hadn't been getting any sleep. I was well and truly losing the battle to stay sane in my insane world.

A few days later, Mum and Grandma had a huge fight. I was surprised it didn't happen earlier. I then became the target of their unhappiness. I was already tired, stressed, depressed and anxious. I didn't need these two grown women including me in their lifelong battle. I packed my bags and left, driving back to the Sunshine Coast on my own. *They can all find their own way home*. Two months later, Grandma had a stroke and died. We never know what is around the corner, do we?

Even in death, Mum wasn't having Grandma around her. I was to keep Grandma's ashes with me until months later, when Mum decided we would have a little get-together to scatter her ashes. I truly believe Grandma knew she wouldn't be welcome in Queensland after the altercation she'd had with Mum. Leaving the planet beforehand was her way of bowing out on her own terms.

By late 1998, only a couple of smaller properties were left. We had an appointment with the assets restructuring department in Brisbane. Beforehand, I had posted to our contact all the fax receipts showing how many real estate agencies I had liaised with regarding our properties for sale, along with diarised copies of everything I had done to try and get everything sold.

I wondered why I had to go to all the trouble of getting this information to him before our appointment. Unbeknown to me, the local bank manager had been in his ear, telling him we didn't want to sell anything and we were ignoring everything the bank had told us we needed to do. Why he thought that I do not know. This idiot of a man had no idea the lengths I went to trying to fix our financial situation. Doing his due diligence, the manager in Brisbane wanted to see what I had been doing, if anything, to sell the properties.

This is it – we will be thrown out on the street, I thought as we pulled into the department car park. *There is nothing more I can physically do.* We rode the lift to the assets restructuring floor. The receptionist directed us to a small group of chairs.

"Would you please take a seat? He will be with you shortly."

Sitting, staring out the window, I wished I was one of the many people below me, scurrying around like ants, instead of sitting here trying not to hyperventilate. *Take deep breaths, in one, two, three, four, out one, two, three, four.* My mind was thinking of all the ways a person could be drawn and quartered.

Like a cat on a hot tin roof,
I couldn't sit still.

I crossed my legs, uncrossed my legs, scratched many nervous itches while trying to look like I was cool as a cucumber.

The receptionist appeared and ushered us into the manager's office. It was a pleasant enough room with a view of the neighbouring buildings. The sun was shining outside, but the room felt cold as ice to me. Smiling awkwardly, we exchanged pleasantries before sitting down. We were then given a spiel about the bank's procedures regarding our predicament. I was sweating profusely, hoping I wouldn't vomit from sheer terror all over this man's solid wooden desk. The next few sentences that came out of his mouth were so unexpected.

"Mrs Wilcox, I can see that you have done everything humanly possible to get your properties sold and reduce the debt. There are only a couple of small properties still for sale, the principal money borrowed has been paid, and there is only some bank interest still owing. I would like to inform you that the bank is willing to forgive the debt which is owing. This decision has been solely made on the extraordinary lengths you went to, Mrs Wilcox, to try and pay off your and your husband's debt."

My mind was racing. I couldn't catch my breath. *What does "forgive the debt" mean? Am I still going to jail?*

"I am sorry, but I do not understand what 'forgive the debt' means. Can you please explain that to me?"

"Well, you and your husband still owe over $250,000 in interest, but you do not have to pay this money back." He then made what I thought to be a funny gesture for a bank manager, smiling and giving me the thumbs-up. “But if by chance you win Lotto in the future, you can repay the favour by sharing your winnings with the bank.”

I was dumbfounded. *Did I just hear him correctly? Is this nightmare finally over?*

Many pieces of paper were signed and hands shaken as I thanked this amazing man many times for the bank’s generosity. A miracle of mega proportions had just happened.

I made it out of his office, back down the lift and back to the car before I burst into tears. My husband was understandably relieved as well. We drove home in silence, too overwhelmed and exhausted to speak. It would take the full trip home for us to process what had just happened.

Eventually the remaining properties were sold, so a little bit more was paid off our forgiven debt. I had never heard the expression “forgive the debt” before that day. What a beautiful phrase. Three small words that can change a person’s life trajectory in an instant.

A couple of weeks had gone past. Life was good. *Nothing can top how happy and grateful I feel.* I was wrong. A visit from my wonderful daughter and her partner left me crying tears of joy... I was going to be a grandma.

CHAPTER 10

A child most blessed

A child is a wondrous being, you might say
Created by God to give love all day long
Two legs, two arms and a mischievous way
Makes you laugh 'til you cry, when they burst into song
Skinned knees, broken bones and some tears you will see
As they grow bigger and bigger, and get their first job
A girlfriend or boyfriend is next, oh dear me
Then without warning, home they will lob
Wedding bells you will hear, and your tears will flow
As down the aisle they will walk, with the love of their life
All dressed in their best, and sitting in a row
You look at them lovingly, and think how they used to get into strife
You hear the news, a baby is expecting
Nine months of waiting to have a cuddle
Before you know it, the little one is sitting
Your grandchild you adore, even the puddles
A child is a wondrous being, you might say

—Jo Wilcox

I was working full-time, enjoying my weekly pay packet, while finalising bookwork relating to the sale of all the properties, filing everything in archive boxes and storing them away. The end had finally come to another soul-destroying episode in my life. We were still moving from one rented property to another, but it didn't seem so bad as I was also watching my daughter's belly expand with every passing month. I was over the moon to be an expectant grandma.

During the time I was fighting for my financial life, my husband had been approached by a wholesale milk distribution franchise he had worked for in his earlier working life. They were re-establishing the franchise areas on the coast after the de-regulation of the milk industry, and they wanted him to take on an area. The franchise agreement would include my husband, myself and partners, all having equal shares in the business.

My gut was doing cartwheels. *I don't want to be a partner in this business.* I could see disaster written all over it. I was enjoying having a regular pay cheque, and the little bit of freedom that afforded me. It was mine. After many discussions with my husband and trying to explain my feelings around this endeavour, he said, "But I need you to do the bookwork."

The wound of always doing what I am told, what others want, overshadowed my desire to stay as far away as I could.

I was talked around to quitting my job again and being tethered to something I didn't want to have any part of. My abuse triggers were still forefront in my mind, leading me to choose a fawn response. I didn't fight. I complied, leaving me with guilt because I didn't stand up for myself. The shame that I was already holding on to grew to humiliating heights. I had shown myself what a coward I was once again.

The milk business officially started near the end of 1998. Here I was again learning business processes, new computer and accounting systems on the fly, out of my depth and hating it. My schooling only went to Year Ten. I had no university or TAFE courses under my belt, so I learnt by doing. I wasn't a happy camper. My migraines had ramped up, causing me all sorts of problems, lost time, pain and truckloads of anxiety.

My heart is pounding with excitement and relief as I answer the telephone. *My first grandchild is on the way!*

Well, what a way to start the day. After being woken with a start, it takes me two goes to place the receiver snugly in the concave telephone holder. Coordination eludes me as I stumble awkwardly across the carpet to negotiate the ensuite doorway. With excitement and apprehension coursing through my body, I quickly shower, dress and grab a bite to eat.

I am smiling like a Cheshire cat as I drive out the gate, my heart full of love for my soon-to-be-born grandchild.

While driving along the well-worn highway, the early-morning traffic races, like columns of ants, nose to tail, heading for the workers' mound. It is June. The sun is creeping slowly over the horizon. The air is crisp. A magical shimmer is coming from patches of frost nestled in gutters along the road. *What a beautiful day to be born.* It's 1999, the last exhausting year of the 20th century before the dawn of the new millennium.

Winding around the levels of the hospital car park, I remember the day my daughter announced she was pregnant, as well as the thrill of being asked to be present at the birth. I park, lock the car and start to walk towards the lifts. The familiar antiseptic smell wafts around me. My blue sneakers on the highly polished floor are noise makers as I walk excitedly to be with Kylie and Brett for the birth of their first child.

I don't know what to expect as I haven't been in a maternity ward since I've had my children. Thankfully, there is no sterile delivery room reeking of antiseptic, where the moans of other ladies are heard through paper-thin walls void of pictures. Or stirrups hanging menacingly. No cotton slippers, hair nets or horrifying instruments, as well as the total disregard for another human being's privacy.

Instead, soothing aromas waft through the beautifully decorated room. Bean bags and large rubber balls take the place of stirrups. A door, which can be closed, affords the expectant mother privacy and peace.

I put my stuff on the floor and gave big hugs to the expectant parents. Kylie is in good spirits and very happy to see me. My excitement is effervescent. Happy tears lovingly trickle like warm honey over my cheeks. The baby's head is engaged. *Not long now.* A few more pushes and my beautiful granddaughter, Hannah, is born.

I will never forget the astonished look on Brett's face when he is handed his little bundle of human emotions with all her fingers and toes. I am overwhelmed, to say the least. I am handed my beautiful granddaughter to cuddle while the happy parents hug each other.

"Hello, my beautiful little girl, I am your grandma. I am so happy to meet you. I love you lots and lots."

I have a long and loving cuddle, and then reluctantly hand her back to her parents. To be part of such a loving experience is beyond words. I am truly blessed.

Grandkids are the best. Hannah and I were constant companions. With her mum and dad working full-time, and me being self-employed, I had the time to mind her. My office was at home, so the arrangement was great for us all. We went to the beach and played in the park. The ladies at the bank knew her by name as we were frequent customers.

My parents had also moved to their new unit in a retirement village on the Sunshine Coast. It was a busy time for me, helping them unpack and get settled, running errands and being the all-round "gofer". And of course, they were great-grandparents now.

Helping my daughter with my new granddaughter gave me a welcomed and loving distraction, and the strength to keep going.

The first time DID was brought to my attention was in 1999. Kylie was visiting and told me about an Oprah Winfrey episode she had watched about a gentleman who had written a book on multiple personalities. It was called *First Person Plural: My Life As A Multiple* by Cameron West, PhD. Kylie went on to explain this man's story and how he changed as his alters, as they were called back then, emerged and took over his day-to-day life. It was fascinating to hear about this man's life and what his coping mechanisms were.

Kylie then very lovingly looked at me and said, "I know what is wrong with you, Mum." At first, I wasn't quite sure what she meant. I had no recollection of having episodes, especially like the ones Cameron had shared. Well, not to my conscious knowledge anyway. Kylie proceeded to tell me about a time when I had lost it at home. "You got really angry, Mum, and your face and voice changed." I didn't know how to react. I had no reason to disbelieve my daughter. My love for her was absolute and I knew she loved me also.

It took a little while for this information to sink in. My head was in turmoil. My logical mind was fighting desperately to make sense of the situation. *This is not me. I don't behave like that. I know what I am doing. I am not insane. I don't have a mental problem. I couldn't have got this far in my life if I was possessed.* I went and bought Cameron's book. My reaction to his story was overwhelming. My attitude changed dramatically, bringing in a lot of doubt around my reality. *Could this be why I don't remember stuff? Is this book the answer to a lot of the questions I have about myself? Shit! What do I do now?*

Over the following weeks, I was gripped by absolute fear and soul-destroying guilt. *Have I done things... bad things... that I don't remember? I hope I haven't hurt my kids over the years and not known I have.* I couldn't console myself. I was so scared. I started to remember things that had happened over the years. Things that I had no explanation for. *Could this be true? Do I suffer from DID?* I kept living my life, not knowing where to turn for help. I pushed these thoughts to the back of my mind.

The following year, I was having a massage and some energy healing work done. I was laying on the massage table. I needed to go to the toilet. The lady walked with me, to show me where her bathroom was. I was feeling really weird. I started to talk like a child. The lady noticed this and stayed with me. As I grappled with my undies and slacks, trying to get them in the upward direction, my mind was racing. I was hearing voices that were not mine. I couldn't control the verbal dialogue. Feeling like I was a very small child, I tried to open the toilet door. An action I have done a trillion times, but at that moment I was struggling. Walking back to her room, as she told me later, I had changed again, with a different voice and mannerisms. After she sat me down and spoke with me at length about what had happened, I was consumed by fear again. My mind was racing, my palms were sweating and I started to cry. The overwhelming recognition that I may have DID was horrifying.

Over a couple of years, a number of personalities, which are called "parts" now, emerged. They all had different mannerisms. Because they never told us their names, if they had any, we gave them proper people names, so we knew who was who in the zoo. My massage therapist was not a psychologist or a medical professional, so we were winging it. We made a list of the parts that visited her, along with names and ages that felt appropriate for each one.

I mapped out:

- Testy Tess – 11 years old
- Jack and Jill (twins) – 13 years old
- Scaredy Cat – 13 years old
- Nasty Nellie – 14 years old
- Sweet Sally – 22 years old
- Competent Cate – 27 years old
- Tired Terri – 29 years old
- Wicked Wendy – 30 years old
- Baby Blue Eyes – 38 years old

Today, my understanding of DID has shed a lot of light on my impressive list of characters who have shared my body and mind for many years.

All of these parts played a role in helping me navigate my unpredictable life.

Over time, either during sessions with my psychologist or during dissociative episodes while I was on my own, I have discovered where their presence has helped me cope with my many struggles and traumas.

The first part who presented was 13-year-old Scaredy Cat. I don't remember what she said – only that she was very upset and frightened, scared enough to want to run away. Nasty Nellie, who is 14, helped me cope during my teenage years, including standing up for myself at home and at school.

My parts could also be problem solvers. When my first marriage was on the rocks, 22-year-old Sweet Sally tried her best to love my first husband unconditionally, hoping he would forgo his love of drink and love me more. Baby Blue Eyes, who is 38, had the same role with my current husband, hoping he would listen to me regarding our financial woes. Each part did their absolute best, but the male ego won out in each instance.

Tired Terri's 29-year-old tenacity, and willingness to work hard to provide for my children when we were a family of three, gave me the strength to hold down four jobs at a time.

I will never forget the many times I laid on the massage table, having a conversation in different voices. On one occasion, I was absolutely amazed and terrified listening to myself talk in two different young voices as the mischievous 13-year-old twins, Jack and Jill, spoke to each other, and it made sense. This playful pair distracted me when Mum and Dad were fighting, blocking the scary noises as best they could.

When I was a kid, 11-year-old Testy Tess helped my cope with the neighbourhood boys' antics.

Between 2000 and 2002, when I met the different parts of me, I was a very different person. I was angry, overwhelmed and tortured by my realisation, whether it was true or not, that I was a raving lunatic. A thought I had all my life. Luckily, I had read Cameron West's book before these parts presented themselves. Even though my parts presenting themselves was very real, and I had a witness, I wasn't convinced. I had no desire to seek information or professional help. I was scared of what people would think of me if they knew. *If I dissociated when I was getting groceries, would they lock me in a mental institution? No way is this real. It is a very vivid dream and I will wake up one day.* Another secret kept under wraps.

Denial ate away at my truth, leaving me unwilling to accept myself as the new poster girl for DID.

Time passed and I was finally proficient in handling the business bookwork. My renting days were over as we had purchased our own home – a beautiful, modest house on seven acres. I loved the space around me. I found it extremely triggering to live in suburbia. The noises from close neighbours' family lives, whether they were happy or scary, kept me in a constant state of hypervigilance, which meant my anxiety levels were always high.

My life was hectic. My old foes, depression and anxiety, were still centre stage in my life, causing havoc wherever they could. But keeping busy was my saving grace, helping to subdue the negative self-talk.

2002 saw another grandchild on the way. Hannah would walk around sticking out her tummy, pretending she was like Mummy, having a baby. I welcomed my first grandson, Oscar. So now I had two little partners in crime. I loved it! More play, more wonderful messes and, of course, more kisses and hugs. The three musketeers wreaking happy havoc wherever we went.

The business was humming along, and we were enjoying having our own home full of our grandchildren's laughter and happiness. Unfortunately, my mum was diagnosed with Alzheimer's. Dad managed to care for her for a few years before we had to put her into care, which was a very stressful situation for us all.

In March 2006, we welcomed another grandchild. This time I was chief babysitter for Hannah and Oscar, while Kylie and Brett were in hospital. We all visited Mummy, Daddy and Archie, their new baby brother in hospital. Seeing my three grandkids have beautiful cuddles together was something I will never forget.

Grandma and her brood of three loving grandkids was what my life was all about. The best medicine for someone who wasn't privy to a safe and loving childhood. We played, swam, climbed trees, cooked, laughed, sang and spent happy, peaceful times together.

CHAPTER 11

Changes

Giving up becomes the way to self-preservation
Giving up becomes the way to hurting less
Giving up becomes the way to encourage rest
But what will tomorrow bring if you give up today?

—Jo Wilcox

Mum was deteriorating. After a fall while she was in care, she was admitted to hospital, where she passed away in July 2006. After Mum passed, Dad said to me, "It's my fault your mother got Alzheimer's. It was because of the way I treated her." He was crying and so remorseful. When alcohol gets a hold of you, it changes who you are, and not in a good way.

I asked a psychologist once if moving Mum to a retirement village would help her. I thought it would be good because most of them had facilities like a pool (she grew up at the beach and loved swimming) and a hall with regular activities, so she could make some friends. His response was, "It doesn't matter where your mum lives. She will always be the same unless she seeks professional help."

I understood that. I am the same. My mental problems are the same no matter what roof I have over my head. It is just the nature of the beast. Mum and I have both been destroyed by our childhoods.

Our struggle is not with bricks and mortar.
Therefore, bricks and mortar will not heal us.

I loved my mum but my love for her was always guarded. I am sure both of us were too frightened to show our feelings. Demonstrating unconditional love to each other was difficult. There was definitely a barrier between us. I wished Mum was more approachable. She was never very maternal.

Even when my children were born, Mum was wary of showing them too much love. Dad on the other hand loved babies and small children.

Sharing cuddles and kisses, rocking them to sleep and playing with them was beautiful to witness.

The closest moments I had with my mum was when she had Alzheimer's. A horrendous disease that robs its host of so much. In Mum's case, though, it softened her personality. I would take Mum on many outings, including ten-pin bowling. Mum loved it and was very good. I was shown more love and understanding from my mum in the last few years of her life than my whole lifetime spent with her. I am forever grateful that I had this loving time with her, even if she wasn't sure who I was most of the time. I would like to think that what I was witnessing was my real mum, her heart open and not afraid.

Having the desire to grow, to leave behind our destructive history, is the only way to combat the evil that was done to us. Unfortunately, it was too late for my mum. Her generation abandoned her. But I am hoping that my generation has learnt from past mistakes. That this generation now, and others to come, will be more tolerant of things they may not fully understand.

Hannah, Oscar and Archie were the only constants in my life. Drop-offs and pick-ups at kindy soon became pre-school, then primary school. I volunteered in their classrooms, went on class excursions. Cheered them all on at swimming and sports carnivals. Hosted birthday parties at home for them and their mates. Still having to do business stuff while the grandkids were with me, they learnt how to count coins and notes. I had little piles of coins all over my desk until they decided to knock them down and start all over again.

After school they would have afternoon tea, and I helped them with their homework. They were showered and all ready for their mum when she came to pick them up to go home. Happiness and unconditional love exploded out of my heart when my adorable grandkids were with me.

My life changed for the better when my grandchildren were born. They afforded me the time and safety to let my inner child be free to explore without fear.

My young life being what it was didn't lend itself to innocent play, exploring, creating or just being happy. My grandchildren gave me the opportunity to be silly, to laugh a lot, to joke around, and to create a time of safe and peaceful togetherness.

I made playdough, slimy goo, paint and coloured glue. Always messes made with love. Always curiosity and playful abandon filling our day. I loved it. It was my happy time, when my inner child would come out to play.

When the grandkids were little, they would sleep over. Before bedtime, we would all pile into my queen-sized bed to have our dessert. I didn't have a TV – I had an old computer monitor and DVD player. There we were, all safe and cosy in bed, watching a screen so small that we almost needed a magnifying glass to see it. But we didn't care. We cuddled, tickled, laughed, chatted and just loved each other. As Hannah, Oscar and Archie got older and bigger, there wasn't room in my bed for us all. Not allowing this to deter me, I moved a lounge chair into my bedroom.

Just like the children's nursery rhyme, *Ten In The Bed*: *And the little one said: "Roll over, roll over." So, they all rolled over and one fell out. There were nine in the bed...* That was us. One rolled over onto the lounge chair. The grandkids would take turns.

We continued having our dessert in my bedroom, together, loving every minute of it, until even my bed and the lounge chair could no longer contain us as my grandchildren continued to grow. Then, we moved into the lounge room. My heart was broken. They were growing up too quickly, but I was still the most loved grandma alive, which was awesome.

My grown-up grandkids still visit, sleep over and love being with their grandma. You may ask about the bed situation. Unfortunately, my traumas led to my husband and I having separate bedrooms. It is what it is.

We all know the TV show *My Kitchen Rules*. Well, there is also my home-grown show, called *Grandma's Kitchen Rules*. The grandkids and I loved to cook together – more mess, more fun. Cooking is fun, especially if it is done with people you love. Right?

The grandkids and I would get together, gathering all my cookbooks and perusing all the recipes. My grandkids' mission, if they chose to accept it, was to each pick three recipes for three dishes: entrée, main and dessert. Then, to cook up a storm and present said recipes for human consumption, with grandma and granddad the human consumptionees (not a word, I know, but it is fun). Assuming the consumptionees survived the tasting, a winner would be chosen. *My* mission, if I chose to accept it, was to go to the $2 shop and find some prizes to be awarded to the winner. (Really, I would be giving prizes to everyone. I couldn't choose one grandchild over another.)

On one occasion, following recipe selection, my shopping list of ingredients was particularly long. *This is going to be so much fun.* The grandkids were around 12, 10 and six. I was hired by the youngest chef to assist with cooking and cleanup for the princely sum of many hugs throughout the day. Accepting this honour, I quickly became the bowl holder, the reader of recipes, the oven controller, the cutter-upperer and the washer-upperer (more fun, made-up words).

The moment of truth arrived when entrées were placed delicately on the plate and served to the nervous consumptionees. Then came the main course – so many flavours, so much food. Granddad and I ploughed through the amazing delicacies in front of us. Finally, dessert. So far, the competition had produced many winning dishes. The chefs were neck and neck. Dessert was another story. Hannah had chosen avocado chocolate mousse. *Yum... not.* We all had a taste, and it was unanimously decided that this recipe wasn't worthy of a thumbs-up. Many crazy cheap prizes were handed out at the awards ceremony. Laughter, happiness and love enveloped all of us. A truly amazing memory that I visit often and will cherish forever.

Meanwhile, things were going on in the business that I wasn't happy with. I had many discussions with my husband regarding my concerns, but they fell on deaf ears, leaving the bad business decisions to multiply exponentially. Cash-flow problems were a result, causing friction in our marriage. The mixed bag of emotions that came with Mum's passing was difficult for me to navigate. My migraines were relentless, causing more anxiety and frustration. Drinking crept back into my life, but only when the grandkids weren't with me.

My grandkids were my little bit of peace and joyfulness in a world of male egos and more financial problems, but even they were not enough to stop me from expressing my anger and frustration when I was on my own, at how the business was being managed. I had many bouts of extreme rage, throwing printers and smashing them, followed by debilitating shame and guilt at my actions, as well as more financial stress, as I had to replace the broken items. My anger just kept escalating to the point of no return. I smashed wall phone handsets after receiving business news I wasn't happy about and I ripped my sliding bedroom door off its tracks, and then I had to try and fix the bloody thing. I was out of control.

I questioned my sanity. *You are a bloody psycho. You should be locked up. Why do you do these horrible things? Why do you get so angry?*

Weekend barbeques on the deck, overlooking our pool and beautiful acreage, ended with me consuming bottle after bottle of wine after my husband went to bed.

My anger was masking my compounding fear – fear that I was going to lose everything again.

Nobody is listening to me. I had been triggered by the immense pressure of our financial problems once again. Anxiety and depression pushed me further and further away from my husband. *My safe place is my bedroom. No one can hurt me if I stay out of the way.* I chose to be sexually inactive to keep myself safe. My bedroom became my TV room as well as my sanctuary. My husband respected my wishes. I had spoken to him about my childhood and my parents. His love for me shone through when he was able to protect me from myself.

What do you do when the low that is your norm falls below freezing? What do you do when any sparks of normal you thought may exist in your universe turn out to be apparitions. My day can change in an instant. The unpredictability of my past photobombing my present is a constant concern. Happiness can unravel into a hidden torment, while my mind becomes a prisoner of another unknown secret. The feelings are real while the reasons are obscured.

My enormous fear led to my second suicide attempt in 2010. More booze and pills, more throwing up. Familiarity breeds contempt. Knowing myself as I do, my contempt grows as I find fault and worthlessness in all that I do. My consideration for my own existence pales against the enormous pull to exit my life of pain.

My life is ruled by past traumas, symptoms fuelled by present-day annoyances, leaving my future dictated by unknown fear and instability.

Dad visited most weekends, enjoying a meal and sleeping over. He was still drinking rum. With all the business upheaval that was my life, having to deal with Dad's drinking as well sent my nervous system into overload. He wanted me to drink with him, but I couldn't. I made up excuses and went to bed, leaving my husband and dad to their drinking.

In March 2012, Dad passed away after battling cancer. Sorting out his funeral and financial affairs took its toll. We had a turbulent life together but I always loved him. I know with all my heart that he loved me too.

A few years later, our partners left the business. Their decision was good and bad. The business didn't have to support them anymore, but we had to find the money to pay them out, putting more pressure on an already exhausted business. Legal documents were drawn up, and monthly payments were the solution.

Unfortunately, Kylie and Brett separated around that time too. Kylie stayed on the coast with my grandkids and Brett moved to Brisbane.

After seeing how Kylie and Guy's father treated them after we separated and he met another lady, I wanted to make sure my grandkids didn't have the same experience. I was happy to take them to see their dad as often as I could. Thankfully, Brett wanted to stay in his children's lives, seeing them weekends as well as school holidays. Brett is a very supportive and loving father.

The business my husband and I had owned for over 17 years was floundering. We had no option but to sell our seven-acre property and downsize to try and manage cash flow and reduce our debt. Our franchisor losing the tender for the supermarket contracts, which were a large portion of our yearly income, was devastating. Paying out the partners along with numerous other negatives, made it almost impossible to keep the day-to-day running on an even keel.

During the process of selling and buying, everything that could go wrong did go wrong. Our bank didn't get the paperwork done in time for our settlement date. The buyers were pissed, understandably. I was told this the day our removalists were already at our house. The settlement of the house we were buying was also delayed. Apparently, the seller's bank lost the deed to the house. I have no idea if that is a thing, but I was absolutely ready to take matters into my own hands and tear strips off someone. The settlement dates no longer matched up. We had no house to move into and we had already moved out of the house we were selling.

A lot of urgent, frantic phone calls later and I was able to get our furniture into storage. My son, Guy, and his partner, Sarah, were able to accommodate us for as long as we needed. *It is all my fault. I must have done something wrong. I am a bloody waste of space. I should be dead.* My past was again intruding in my present, causing me to react negatively to the situation, even though all the things that were happening had absolutely nothing to do with me. I could not have stuffed this up.

But wait, there's more...

Two weeks after we moved in with Guy and Sarah, the bank called, telling me we were allowed to move into the house we were buying. Wonderful news. But we had to pay rent until the deed and adjacent paperwork were finalised. We were not allowed to hang a photo or put up a fence because we were renting our own home, which we had already paid for. My anxiety was overwhelming and my anger was destroying my ability to think straight. I was so sceptical of my ability to ride out this horrendous scenario. All my feelings of self-doubt, worthlessness and being out of control bubbled to the surface.

I was a volcano just waiting to erupt, and heaven help anyone who was within the fallout area.

The hits kept coming. We had a beautiful Golden Labrador named Silver. He was the cutest puppy when I bought him from a pet shop. He was nine years old, a beautiful gentle soul, my constant companion. I had already organised to have a fence put up for Silver. Now that was not going to happen. Not being able to keep my dog safe was the last straw. Guy and Sarah were wonderful and said that Silver could stay with them until we could put the fence up. I was so grateful. We got our furniture out of storage and moved in. But remember, we were paying rent at this stage. We quickly erected a makeshift fence, using milk crates tied together. Thank goodness it was only a small area that needed to be fenced. Silver could come home to me.

But wait, there's still more...

The seller's bank finally produced a workable deed for the house we were buying. I thought: *this is it – we will finally own our home.*

Don't hold your breath!

I received a phone call from my bank just after we moved into our new rented home. He told me there was not enough money to buy the house we were already living in. This was bullshit. I had more than one appointment with the bank regarding all of this. I was livid and, at the same time, I wanted to just curl up in bed and cry. This man also asked me if I knew a certain lady.

"Yes. She is my daughter, Kylie."

"Should she have been given $30,000?"

"Ah, no. She has nothing to do with this."

When I heard this, my heart began to beat frantically in my chest, my palms were sweating, and I felt physically sick. The anger that was welling up inside of me was sitting behind my teeth, just waiting for me to open my mouth so I could spew out as many swear words as I could think of. So, on top of everything else, the bank had given my money away. *How could this happen*? Kylie was with me when I received the call. I asked her to look at her bank account, and, sure as eggs, the money was in her account.

I found out later that Kylie was not the only one who received my money. Apparently, it was just human error – someone not doing their job correctly. If Guy and Sarah hadn't come to our rescue, we would have had nowhere to live. Eventually all the money was found. The seller's bank finalised their paperwork, but not until we had paid three weeks in rent.

No one cares that the person on the other end of this ridiculous mistake is suffering tremendously. The atrocious handling of this episode sent me so deep into my black hole that I didn't want to come out. I had given up on life. This led to my third suicide attempt in 2015.

CHAPTER 12

Trapped

I breathe in, I breathe out
Do I have the strength to release a shout?
Will I ever be heard, if I utter a word?
Let me go, let me be free
Will someone ever hear my plea?
My body and mind they interact
Not strong enough
Forever trapped

—Jo Wilcox

Walking down the corridor to my first sexual abuse counselling session, I was confronted with a playroom filled with toys, picture books, teddy bears, colouring books and pencils. All the items were for little ones to come and play with. Tiny tables and chairs were strategically placed around the room, ready for the eager artist to sit and draw a masterpiece. I hadn't thought that child sexual abuse was still happening. Wishful thinking, I suppose. I was devastated, sick and utterly horrified each time I walked past the playroom.

One time, I was so distraught that I spoke to my counsellor about the playroom and how upsetting it was for me. Her response was, "You need to look at this positively. These abused children are here getting professional help. They have had someone listen to them and care enough about them to bring them here. They will learn coping mechanisms. And in a lot of cases, their abuser has been charged, and they won't be hurt anymore. Not like your experience of not having anyone to help you." When I looked at it that way, I felt better but still horrified that these little ones had been hurt.

I see you. No one has ever said to me, "I see you."

My counselling sessions continued. One day, I was sitting across from my counsellor when I started to feel strange. I stared intimidatingly at her and pronounced, "You will never know our secret." I was confused, not knowing what had just happened. My counsellor asked, "Are you okay? Do you want to continue with our session?" I answered "Yes" to both questions.

I understand now that I had a dissociative episode.

I received a lot of valuable information at my counselling sessions. I learnt that child sexual abuse will trigger the mind and body to become hypervigilant, as a form of protection, to keep you safe. My hypervigilance led to extreme sensitivities to noises, smells, medications and sometimes just everyday life.

My sensitivities include car and strong chemical fumes, which make me feel sick. The smell of coffee, meat cooking and cigarette smoke agitate me. I hate winter because of the chimney smoke, and spring and summer aren't much better because of the controlled burns and barbeques. Loud sudden noises send me into panic, sometimes screaming and hiding. On really bad days all I can do is shut my house up and hope for the best.

I also learnt that a child molester will groom their prey. A child molester is a cunning, ritualistic individual. You have to remember that I was in my sixties when I was given information regarding child sexual abuse. Before this, I had no idea that my symptoms and behaviours were all the aftermath of being abused as a small child.

On one hand, I was relieved because I finally understood why I was the person I was.

But on the other hand, I was riddled with guilt, and I was angry, very angry, mainly at myself. I couldn't understand why I allowed this man to do the things he did. This was a big one for me. It took a lot of sessions for me to soften the debilitating self-loathing I had. To this day, I can easily return to that self-loathing, which escalates into blaming myself for every damn thing that has happened to me.

There is an amazing group of ladies who are members of a quilters club. They work tirelessly to distribute handmade patchwork quilts to many helpful organisations. I have been given two of their beautiful quilts over the years I have been going to counselling. These quilts take pride of place in my home They are a reminder of how far I have come in my journey to heal, and the caring and helpful people I have met along the way.

Healing is extremely emotional and can be hard to navigate at times. My inner child has been damaged and is scared – she just wants to be kept safe from her perceived threats. My inner teenager has one emotion, which is anger, and she wants someone to pay for how she was treated. My adult self just wants peace. She is exhausted from fighting.

Having DID and being at the mercy of my parts can sometimes put me in a volatile situation. The following is a prime example.

My peace was shattered when Miss Angry, who is my protector, crashed a family gathering I was attending. This incident happened way before I knew I had DID. I remember because I was consciously present, but I wish it never happened.

It was in the early 1980s. My family and my sisters' families were visiting our parents. We all had young children. Dad was cooking a barbeque for lunch. Most of us had been swimming in the pool. Everyone was having a great time. Laughter and silliness abounded. It was time for lunch. I was feeling uneasy. The smells of cigarette smoke, barbeque meat and Dad drinking rum were all starting to trigger me.

One minute I was eating lunch, the next I was yelling at my niece, Katherine. Dad was serving prawns. My sisters and I were always worried about what would happen if our kids didn't eat what Dad cooked, especially if he had been drinking. Katherine didn't like prawns. I feel my outburst was triggered by what Dad might do when Katherine refused to eat the prawns.

Because of my history with Dad, Miss Angry was protecting me from what she thought would happen to me if Dad became angry. I couldn't stop myself from berating my little niece. It was horrific hearing me upset an innocent child. A child that I loved. My eyes could see the horrified looks on my family's faces. I wanted to apologise to everyone. I wanted to stop whatever was happening and hug my niece. I couldn't move. I couldn't say the words I wanted to say. The rage in my father's eyes as he approached me made me feel like I was going to throw up. There was no backing down. No matter how hard I tried to stop yelling, I couldn't. My fate was sealed. *Today, my father will knock me out. I am done.* All I could do was give in, allowing Miss Angry to do her worst.

My father dragged me, still yelling, away from the table. Mum and Dad both had to try and calm me down. It probably didn't help that it was Dad in my face trying to settle me. Miss Angry only got more verbally abusive. Now the spewing out of ugly remarks were directed at my parents. My logical mind was telling me: *settle down, don't say anything, don't upset Dad. You know what will happen if you make him mad.*

What started as an intervention quickly became a fight to the death, as far as Miss Angry was concerned. She was relentless.

All the things I had wanted to say to my mother and father for years spilled from my mouth. There was no resistance. Of course, the more Miss Angry persisted, the worse the reaction from my parents was. My parents were full of alcohol, and I was full of rage and pent-up emotions. It was not a healthy combination.

A slap across my face from my father was the only thing that snapped me out of my resentment-filled temper. I wasn't the most loved person at our family barbeque after that. And I don't blame anyone for their reactions.

When I decided to write my book, I contacted Katherine and talked to her about this episode. We had a lovely lunch together. I apologised for my actions and the hurt I caused her. She was very understanding. During our conversation, Katherine told me, "Aunty Jo, you can go from being so loving and happy to dreadfully angry and intimidating very quickly." *Oh, my goodness.* My heart sank.

I have tried to cope by dissociating all my life, not understanding what I was doing. Sometimes I know what is going on when a part presents itself. My psychologist calls it "being present". Other times, I am absolutely unaware that I have dissociated and am oblivious to what is happening around me. On occasion, I lose sense of time and don't even know where I am or how I got there. In the case of the ill-fated family barbeque, I understand now that horrible episode in my life wasn't me. I would never hurt my niece like that. But in my eyes, it *was* me – the frustrated, unloved, put-down and unwanted me – getting revenge the only way she knew how.

For years, Miss Angry was the one who gave me the strength to retaliate against Dad. She was the owner of *The Look* which I gave to Dad on many occasions, with dire consequences for me. She had an accomplice. There was another part who emerged at a session to relive the memory of me punching Dad. His name was Tommy. He was 16 years old. I do not have many parts who actually name themselves. He was very aggressive and had helped keep me safe, and to stand up to bullies. He was the one who marched me out of my bedroom and planted me in front of my dad. Tommy's aggressive nature was not helpful to me as I got older. During the session, my psychologist explained to him, he could be assertive and strong in present time without needing to be aggressive.

My parts have guided my life for many years, keeping me safe from perceived threats. They are holding memories of abuse, suffering and sheer terror. They are petrified, so I am petrified. The Eye Movement Desensitisation and Reprocessing (EMDR) work that I do with my psychologist helps to integrate my parts. EMDR works on the principle that the mind can in fact heal from psychological trauma the same way as our body recovers from physical traumas like cuts and bruises.

It is psychotherapy that helps people heal from the symptoms and emotional distress that are the result of disturbing life experiences. EMDR is what my psychologist uses to help my parts orientate into the now. Helping them to realise they are not still experiencing the trauma. They are safe and their abusers have passed away. They will never be abused again. Adult Jo will protect them.

Over the years, science and technology, along with wonderful medical researchers who want to understand the impact of child sexual abuse, have allowed me to glean knowledge about my diagnoses. This has helped me tremendously. Now I need to put it all together and map out what events in my life led to my DID diagnosis. It is still a relatively new discovery. Sometimes a diagnosis can be a negative thing. But for me, the DID diagnosis has helped me a lot. It fills in a lot of gaps. I now understand my different behaviours. Some have been positive, but, unfortunately, a lot of dissociations have caused me a lot of grief. Yes, understanding why I have acted the way I have over the years has given me a lot of comfort. But there is also still a lot of shame and guilt attached to certain situations.

After being triggered as a child, I would retreat into my bedroom. My fear was overwhelming. All I wanted to do was hide where no one would find me, and I would be safe forever. But this wasn't to be. To cope with the constant upheaval that was my life, another young part was born. We will call her Miss Hide. She hides under a sheet or blanket – this is her protection. My psychologist feels this little part may also be the one who comes to visit but is either preverbal or non-verbal. She has visited more than once.

We have done some work with Miss Hide to help her realise that she is no longer being abused. That she is older now and adult Jo will never let anything happen to her. She is a lot more settled now, but there have been a few instances in the last few years where I have gathered a sheet or blanket out of my linen cupboard and had to cover myself up while watching TV or go to bed and hide under the covers completely. It is upsetting for me, especially when I may not have known why I have fallen back into old habits to protect myself. After many sessions with my psychologist, I am more aware when something has triggered me. I still may not know what it was, but I feel a difference in me. These sessions have helped me to understand why as an adult I would resort to such childlike behaviour.

The cocooning of my fractured soul helps me to feel safe during a time of intense emotional upheaval.

By 2016, I had stopped seeing my psychiatrist as I was settling into seeing my first psychologist and receiving counselling for sexual abuse survivors. I was having a lot of physical problems. My body was starting to break down from the enormous stress that was ever-present in my life.

Oscar and Archie were playing rugby for a team near where their dad lived. Their games were on a Saturday. As Oscar played in the older age bracket, he had rugby training through the week. I would pick him up from school, armed with food, warm clothes, towels and anything else I thought we might need if it was raining, freezing or windy. Afternoon tea would be eaten during our drive down to Brisbane. While Oscar trained, I would have my dinner, which I also brought for us both. After training he changed into warm, dry clothes, setting himself up in the front seat ready to devour his dinner. I would try and have something different each week – hotdogs on bread rolls, savoury mince, beef burgers or a meat stew. The one constant was hot chocolate with marshmallows – Oscar *loved* marshmallows – followed by some form of dessert.

I adored these times with my amazing grandson; just him and me shooting the breeze, talking about personal stuff, school stuff, sport stuff and of course cars. Nothing was off limits. I loved him with all my heart. Oscar would sleep over after training and then in the morning we picked up Hannah and Archie and off to school we went.

As my grandchildren grew, they still slept over through the week and on weekends. We read books together before they went to bed. As they got older, the books changed from picture books to books on cars and question-and-answer books, with them seeing who could find the answer first. We all loved that time together.

The agonising pain in my left arm and shoulder continued through 2016. My arm was starting to shrivel up. I was very worried. I was put on Endone for the pain and sent for some scans. The pain in my arm made it difficult for the technician to do the x-ray. Every move I made caused shooting pain down my arm. We got it done and I was sent off to have an MRI.

Two lovely ladies were waiting for me. I was given instructions regarding the procedure.

"Please lie down on the bed and keep really still. There will be some noise, but it won't take too long. I will talk you through the procedure as we go."

I was shown a button that I could push if I needed to. I was extremely anxious. *You can do this. It will only take a few minutes.*

"Are you okay to start?"

"Yes."

As I was moved into the tunnel, I could hear the noise, which got louder and louder. *It's okay, I can do this. I am safe, I am safe.* I kept trying to reassure myself. Memories were flashing in front of me like bright neon signs, one after the other, of my step-grandfather, Dad. I was petrified. *I want to get out! I want to get out! Let me out! Don't cry. Don't cry.*

A memory of being trapped in the public toilets took my breath away. I hadn't thought about this for a trillion years.

I was around 14 years old. I'd run to the toilets, needing to wee. I opened the stall door, shutting it behind me, pulled down my pants and sat down. Relief. There was a noise above me. I looked up to see a male's face staring down at me over the low stall divider. Within a millisecond, I was in flight mode. Scaredy Cat, whom we met in 2000, wanted to run and run fast. With her help, I pulled up my pants with one hand, opened the door with the other and started to run. I smashed right into him outside the stall door. He pushed me back into the small space, unzipped his pants and exposed his erect penis.

"I've shown you mine, now you show me yours," he snarled.

My heart was pounding so fast. I was crying uncontrollably. He came as close as he could to me, pressing his penis up against me. *He is going to rape me. Run! Run!* So much adrenaline was rushing through my body. He took his eyes off me for a second. *Push him, push him hard! Run, run.* I lunged forward. With all the strength I could muster, I shoved him back out of the stall. He stumbled backwards and fell over. I leapt over him and ran away as fast as I could. I never told anyone what had happened.

Being a keeper of secrets keeps me safe, but at what cost?

Drifting back into the MRI room, I realised I had been pressing the button the lady had given me. I was sweating profusely and started to crawl out of the MRI machine.

"Stop moving, I will bring you out. Stay still."

Time stood still, waiting to come out of that claustrophobic tunnel. It only took those few minutes being inside the machine for me to lose it.

I was crying and shaking like a leaf. The ladies tried to calm me down. I knew I needed to get the MRI if I was going to find out what was wrong with my arm.

A few days later, I had my appointment with the specialist who sent me for the MRI. This man was a pig and had the bedside manner to prove it. He wouldn't look me in the eye. He hated it when I told him I couldn't do the MRI.

"Too bad if you have trouble with it. You have to do it."

"I will go anywhere to have the MRI done as long as I can be sedated."

He thought that was funny. "You have three options: operation, steroid needles while having a scan or tough it out."

"I will tough it out."

"It will get a lot better, and the pain will subside, but the numbness will take a few months. If you don't get better, come and see me again."

Over my dead body am I ever going to see that prick of a man again. As I walked out of his office, I felt sick and so disillusioned. *Why do these sorts of things keep happening to me? Why do I have this sort of male come into my life? I am a good person. I wouldn't hurt anyone deliberately. Am I being punished for something?* It took a few months, but my arm finally came good, and I was free of the pain.

These horrendous things have got to stop happening to me. One positive though: I had stopped drinking, hopefully for good this time.

CHAPTER 13

The calm before the storm

Hope is an emotion of circumstance
We can hope for a sunny day, to find our true love,
to be financially secure, to have good health
When circumstances enter our lives that we cannot control
Hope helps us to fight, no matter the odds

—Jo Wilcox

The day had come for Hannah to do her driving test. After she passed her learner's exam, she wanted to drive everywhere. I was her instructor. We drove to and from school, down the highway and through Brisbane to see her dad. David and Emma from Road Ready on the Sunshine Coast helped Hannah with a few driving lessons. David was so caring and knowledgeable. Hannah and I were both excited and anxious at the same time. She passed. Woohoo. There was no stopping her now. I was so very proud of her. I was 61 years old. *I hope I am not too old and crazy to teach Oscar and Archie how to drive.*

It was school holidays, and the grandkids were helping me put together Silver's new kennel. Silver loved lying in the sun and just chilling. Unfortunately, he was terrified of thunder, so I wanted to be sure he had somewhere to feel safe if I wasn't home to let him into the house. A lot of banging and clanging later and Silver had a new, solid, comfy home. Archie also made a new bowl for his food.

At this time, my GP diagnosed me with Clinical Depression, also known as Major Depressive Disorder (MDD). I asked what the difference between depression and clinical depression was.

"Depression can be mild or severe," my doctor replied. "Mild Depression might only last a few days or weeks, a reaction to an event that is going on in your life. Clinical Depression is a much more severe type. It may last months or even years. Because you have had many events in your life that were traumatic, your depression is ongoing. You have told me that you have feelings of extreme sadness and crying. Your feelings of hopelessness and helplessness cause low self-esteem and worthlessness, because you are always blaming yourself. You are always tired, your sleep pattern is erratic. You have also mentioned how angry and frustrated you get. All of these symptoms have then led you to your suicide attempts. Hopefully through regular visits, we will be able to dampen your symptoms."

After this explanation, I wasn't surprised by my diagnoses. For years I hadn't been able to understand or explain why I felt nothing but disconnection. Why I couldn't get off the roundabout of persistent sadness and hopelessness. My depression runs and ruins my life. It is a cruel manipulative task master. Hiding in plain sight becomes a normal occurrence for me.

I wish my childhood traumas never happened and I could be free of my mental health issues. Unfortunately, trying to help myself feel better, cope better, understand myself better is a long and extremely emotional journey. The unpredictability of myself and my day causes a lot of confusion and instability. Although the more I learn about myself and why I react to things the way I do, is very helpful.

Another little bit of the puzzle fell into place.

Unfortunately, my MDD is "treatment resistant". Because of my allergic reactions to antidepressants over the years, I do not take them. My hypersensitivity continues to let me down.

School was back and it was the first swimming carnival of the summer. My grandkids were all good swimmers, just like their mum and dad. Hannah had graduated Year Twelve the previous year, so I only had my grandsons still at school, Oscar in Year Ten and Archie Year Six.

First up was the primary school carnival. I arrived with my chair, hat, water bottle, snacks and of course my loudest cheering voice. Archie swum really well, while having lots of fun at the same time. When the carnival finished, students were allowed to go home with their parents or caregivers.

“Grandma, can we stay to watch Oscar’s carnival?” Archie asked.

“Yes, of course. That would be great.”

Watching the big kids enter the swimming pool grounds, I snuck a wave to Oscar and he snuck one back. It was a beautiful, sunny day, with teenagers laughing and eating ice blocks while waiting for their names to be called. When Oscar’s name was called, he stood on the block, waiting for the starting pistol to sound the beginning of the race.

In he dived. Archie and I jumped up and started cheering him on. Something was wrong. He was slowing down. I watched as he made his way to the edge of the pool, where he almost passed out. A teacher helped him out of the pool, as he couldn’t finish the race. By the time Oscar reached where I was sitting, he was trying to hide the fact that he was crying. He sat down beside me and broke down.

“Grandma, I don’t feel well.”

As I was holding him, my gut was telling me: *there is something wrong... really wrong*. Oscar was pale – he was not the robust young man I knew. I let the teacher know I was taking both grandsons home. I held him as we all walked to the car. Kylie had said Oscar and Archie could sleep over that night.

“Do you still want to sleep over? I can take you both home if you want.”

"We want to stay with you, Grandma," was their response.

While we were driving home, I tried to get him a doctor's appointment, but they were fully booked. After we got home, I rang Kylie, explained what happened, and told her she needed to make an appointment for Oscar to see a doctor as soon as possible. I was very adamant that he had to have thorough blood tests done.

I have had very good gut instincts in the past and this was no exception.

There is something very wrong with Oscar. Encouragingly, Oscar felt better after we got home. He had a shower, ate dinner, and we all watched a movie and relaxed before going to bed.

I was in constant contact with Kylie before and after the doctor's appointment. We were anxiously waiting for the results.

Early February Kylie received a phone call, asking her to take Oscar to Nambour Hospital, even though there still wasn't an official diagnosis. Archie was in Brisbane visiting his dad, but Brett brought him up. When Brett arrived on the coast, I met him and picked Archie up.

After a few hours at Nambour Hospital, Oscar was transferred to Lady Cilento Children's Hospital in Brisbane. It is now called Queensland Children's Hospital. By the time Oscar, Kylie and Brett arrived at the hospital in Brisbane, he had been diagnosed with Acute Lymphoblastic Leukaemia (ALL).

I will never forget when I was told about Oscar's diagnosis. I had picked up Hannah and Archie. We were in the car, so I pulled over to take the phone call. I was told it is the most common childhood cancer. It happens when a bone marrow cell develops an error in its DNA.

"What is it, Grandma?" Hannah asked.

"Oscar has leukaemia."

I was trying so hard not to cry, to stay strong for my grandkids. Hannah started crying. She understood the severity of Oscar's diagnosis. Archie was 11 years old. I could see from the look on his face that he was confused.

"What is leukaemia, Grandma?"

With tears starting to roll down my face, I said, "It is cancer, sweetheart."

Archie started crying. He understood what cancer was.

"Let's get out of the car so we can have a hug."

We stood on the safe side of the car, crying and hugging each other. I couldn't let go of my precious grandkids. I thought of Oscar and the horrendous journey of healing that was in front of him. *Kylie and Brett will be devastated. How are we all going to get through this? It isn't fair.*

Hannah and Archie slept over that night. We travelled down to Brisbane the next day to see Oscar. He had a room of his own, which was great. By the time we got there, loaded up with snacks for Oscar, the room was full of family. We all came together for our amazing, caring Oscar, showing him he was not alone.

Kylie stayed in the hospital with Oscar as he battled all the horrendous tests and eventually started chemotherapy.

Archie was living with me permanently so his life could be as normal as possible. I was still going to counselling. Nothing was going to distract me from caring for Archie, helping Kylie wherever I could and seeing Oscar as often as possible.

I had my game face on, my mask of resilience placed tightly over my crying eyes.

Archie and I did his homework together. I attended everything he had on and took him to meet his friends after school to skateboard. His friends' mums were a great comfort to me, allowing me to talk about Oscar and have a cry if I needed to. I kept the school informed about Oscar's progress. The school staff were all so caring and helped wherever they could, so Archie and I were in good hands while we navigated our new reality.

A couple of weeks after Oscar was admitted to hospital, he and Kylie were transferred to Clem Jones – Sunland Blood Cancer Centre, in Coopers Plains, Brisbane. That was to be their home away from home for the duration of Oscar's treatment.

It was a great facility with beautiful, landscaped gardens, a patient support centre, games and an activity room, a common room and a gymnasium. Kylie and Oscar couldn't have asked for a more relaxing and well-appointed place to stay in when Oscar wasn't in hospital.

Archie was still playing rugby in Brisbane and off we would go after school on Friday for training, which started at 5:30pm. A couple of times, we were a little late. When Archie went up into the older team, his training wasn't until 6pm, which made a big difference in time management for us. After training, Archie would stay down in Brisbane with his dad and see Oscar.

Archie had his 12th birthday party in March. Kylie came home to celebrate with him while Brett stayed with Oscar. A lot of toing and froing went on, making sure that Kylie could come home for a break and see the rest of her family while another family member would stay with Oscar.

As Oscar's lumbar puncture surgeries showed less leukaemia in his blood, he was allowed to come home to the Sunshine Coast for a weekend. He loved these visits – a little bit of normality in his hectic, painful and stressful life.

The business wasn't going well. Our cash-flow problems were dreadful. In hindsight, we should have sold the business. Instead, the decision was made to sell our home. How stupid could I be? They say you shouldn't make major decisions under stress. I couldn't have been under more stress. My depression had hit an all-time low and my lower back was horribly sore, leaving me no choice but to seek help. Physio treatments made no difference as it was emotional stress that had manifested in my body as a physical ailment.

In May, my dear friend Lyn's life was turned upside down when her husband, Roy, was diagnosed with Non-Hodgkin's Lymphoma. Lyn had been supporting me through my journey with Oscar, but now she had her own horrendous journey to undertake with her husband. I felt helpless that I couldn't physically be there for her because helping my family took up all my time. We kept in touch and supported each other in other ways as best we could. Our many years of close friendship provided both of us with a loving and safe place to land when we needed it.

I proceeded to fall helplessly into my black hole. CPTSD, depression and anxiety were my constant companions, clouding my thoughts, leaving me vulnerable.

I had survivor's guilt. If I could have taken Oscar's place, I would have.

Oscar had many bouts of uncontrollable vomiting, blood noses and high fevers over the four months following his diagnosis. In and out of hospital, chemo and radiation treatments, blood transfusions, every sort of test you could think of, and there was still cancer in his system. His doctor relayed that Oscar would need to have a bone marrow transplant, but not until all the cancer was gone. This was proving to be more difficult than they thought. Oscar's cancer blood count eventually reached a low enough number that his doctor began preparing for the bone marrow transplant.

All family members were instructed to have blood taken to see if anyone was a match to Oscar. Archie was the one. An incredibly big decision for a 12-year-old to make, but there was no hesitation. Archie stepped up, proving to everyone what I already knew – he was a very brave young man.

Oscar was able to come home to the coast for Hannah's 18th birthday and going-away party. Hannah was moving to New South Wales, so far away, and my heart was breaking. The thought of not having her close was unbearable. Oscar and I stayed at Kylie's house while the rest of the family attended the dinner party at a lovely restaurant. With Oscar's bone marrow transplant coming up, he had to be careful of infections, so he stayed away from large crowds. We had our own little celebration with Hannah when she came home. My beautiful granddaughter was going to leave us all for the next chapter of her life.

Transplant day was in July. I had dropped Archie off to his dad the day before as they needed to be at the hospital early. There was no way I wasn't going to be there to support Archie. I arrived at the hospital before 6am and sat waiting for Archie and Brett to arrive. We chatted for a bit until Archie was called into the pre-operative holding area. I received the biggest hug from Archie and a kiss. His eyes told me he was frightened.

"You will be okay. I will be here when you come out, sweetheart. I love you so much."

"Love you too, Grandma."

Brett went with Archie into the pre-operative area. He was Archie's loving support now. Once Archie went into theatre, Brett found me, and we kept each other company until the 90-minute operation was over and Archie came back to the post-operative ward. I was so grateful I was allowed to be with Archie.

The operation was a success. Archie's bone marrow was to go through some testing and then be given to Oscar intravenously. Kylie was with Oscar in the ward upstairs, supporting him through this next stage in his recovery.

I was so happy and relieved to see Archie. I was still having tremendous back pain, so I stood beside his bed, opposite Brett and Archie's step-mum, Iris. The bedside railing was up, so I could lean on it. I needed to touch Archie, but I didn't want to embarrass him. I put my hand under the sheet without anyone noticing and found Archie's hand. He grabbed my hand so tenderly and didn't let go. He knew he was safe and I loved him.

I kept in constant contact by text with Kylie. She was so grateful I was there with Archie. We still had to be mindful of Oscar's low immunity, so Kylie couldn't leave his room to be with Archie. I have the most amazing daughter – she is so resilient. Archie understood why Kylie couldn't be with him. He had made the selfless decision to donate his bone marrow to his big brother. He didn't want anything to harm Oscar's chances of recovery.

By late afternoon, Archie went home with his dad, staying for a few days so he could receive post-operative care. My drive home was extremely emotional. I was crying non-stop. The fear I had for both Oscar and Archie's wellbeing escaped from my fragile body with every tear I cried. I got home from Brisbane around 8:30pm, struggling with horrific lower back pain. I took some painkillers, hoping they would help me sleep.

After a few days Archie was back with me. The top of both his pelvic bones had an incision, where the bone marrow was drawn from, which had to be dressed daily. I was able to take photos of Archie's wounds and send them to his doctor at the hospital, so she could see his healing progress.

We slowly got back into our daily routine: school, work, downtime and sharing lots of love.

CHAPTER 14

Courage

Having the courage to stand my ground,
strong and tall in my conviction,
knowing tomorrow may bring more pain and heartache,
sends a powerful message to those who wish
to keep me downtrodden, closeted.
I am leaving my yesterday with perseverance, moving
through my today with determination,
landing in my tomorrow, knowing my courage
to overcome will forge me a better future.

—Jo Wilcox

Archie had started back at school and his wounds were healing up. Oscar's doctors had finally sorted out his medications and he was recovering slowly. Kylie and Oscar were able to go back to their townhouse, travelling to the hospital for treatment and appointments. That also meant Archie and I could visit Kylie and Oscar regularly. It had been six months since Oscar's diagnosis. What a bumpy ride it had been for us all.

I had started a 12-week compassion-focused therapy (CFT) group program at the same place I went to for sexual abuse counselling. It was the pilot program, which ran from September to October 2017. At one session, we were doing some guided imagery exercises. Before the exercises, we were discussing trauma and it had unsettled me.

Stop. Stop, racing heart, breathe normally. I cannot freak out in front of the group. I don't know these people. Keep it together or they will know your secret. I am so scared.

Closing my eyes to do the guided imagery exercise, which should have been a calming experience for me, triggered memories of being extremely vulnerable and afraid.

What is wrong with me? I cannot open my eyes. What is wrong with my head? It is hanging down. I cannot move it... I cannot move my head. Shit – I am so scared!

"Jo, Jo, it is okay – you are safe. You are safe, Jo."

I think someone is talking to me. I can't hear them properly. Why can't I hear them? Am I going deaf?

I could still faintly hear what was going on around me. I knew someone was talking to me, but I couldn't comprehend what they were saying.

My mouth won't work. Why can't I talk? Shit – now I can't talk. What is wrong with me?

It seemed like a long time before I heard another lady's voice.

"Jo, this is your counsellor. Jo, you are okay. You are safe, Jo. I am here to help you, Jo. Jo, you are safe."

I think I know this person. What is she saying to me?

The more this lady spoke to me, the louder her voice became.

I recognise her voice – she is my counsellor. I can hear what she is saying now. What is going on? I trust her – she will help me.

I started to wriggle in my chair. I had feeling back in my body.

I can see her. I can see the room. I can hold my head up. What just happened? I want to go home.

The facilitator did some grounding exercises for the whole group, making sure we were all okay and happy to carry on with the program.

Afterwards, I spoke with my counsellor and the facilitator of the focus group. I had just experienced a dissociative episode. I had been triggered by what was going on in the group and my brain didn't want to go to the memory – it was too traumatic. To keep me safe, my mind's coping strategy was to dissociate to ensure I didn't have to stay engaged with that memory. It was an extremely surreal feeling, being there but not being there. I had never experienced that before.

I hadn't fainted. I left my body so I couldn't feel.

Another memory emerged during a group counselling session a few weeks later. Throughout the session, I had been wiping my face with my hand. It was like I had walked through a spider web and I was trying to wipe the web off my face. I was getting more and more agitated, more and more animated. The session counsellor noticed what was happening and asked if I was okay. I wasn't, but I didn't know what was happening. I started to cry – I became hysterical. Then the pictures flooded my mind.

I was about three or four years old. My step-grandfather was sitting on a lounge chair, with no pants on. I was standing in front of him, playing with his penis. It was long and hard, and he was making funny noises. Then all of a sudden, stuff squirted all over my face. As an adult now, I understand what had happened to me. This sorry excuse of a human being had ejaculated all over my face. My little, innocent face. The liquid was what I was trying to wipe off my face.

I had no idea this had happened to me before this episode. Crying uncontrollably, I wished I could disappear. But the overwhelm of remembering this memory had me glued to the chair. Reliving every unspeakable second of this traumatic memory as though I was still playing my part in this insidious event. I was also worried that I may have traumatised others in the group. My secret was definitely out, front and centre.

I had spoken to the counsellors previously about what they could do to help me if ever I dissociated. My psychologist told me that when I dissociate and if I am inconsolable, I am to hug myself. My right hand should be placed on the top of my left arm and my left hand on top of my right arm. Then I am to tap each hand alternatively. This is called a butterfly hug. Depending on how distressed I am, the soothing action of the butterfly hug will hopefully not take too long to calm me down.

My psychologist also mentioned because the butterfly hug is a gentler form of bilateral stimulation (activating both sides of the brain) it is very helpful when I am emotionally upset during a session. The tapping is still doing memory reprocessing and will integrate new information. We can also ask parts to feel the tapping which is soothing for everyone. It is also a good tool to use for online sessions, although eye movements can also be used.

The butterfly hug was created and first used with groups of people following disasters, such as earthquakes. In these cases, it was impossible for the therapist to wave their finger (the traditional method of EMDR) in front of all the members of the group. They found that the butterfly hug worked very well for the repossessing of traumatic memories.

It is also very useful outside of therapy, safe and easy to use. It is a simple and effective grounding tool, which helps to calm the stress and anxiety of everyday life. As you are tapping you can, close your eyes, breathe deeply, and add a positive affirmation, if you wish.

If the episode is not too stressful then tapping on the sides of my glasses can also help. Positively affirming that I am safe will also help me orientate back into the present and will soothe the part that is holding the traumatic memory.

After I spoke with my psychologist at my next session about this incident, she asked if this part would like to come forward so she could help her. I have named this little one Miss Brave. She didn't give us her age. The enormous courage it took for this memory to be re-experienced by Miss Brave was incredible. This part of me had been holding this memory since it happened. Keeping me safe from the reality, fearful that I wouldn't have been able to cope when I was little.

It was just as horrifying in session as it was at the counselling group. Being in an absolutely terrified state is no place for a small child to be. EMDR work was performed to relieve Miss Brave of the belittling emotions attached to the memory. Now if this memory comes to the surface, I don't relive the fear. I can sit with it, see it in my mind's eye, but not react.

In August 2017, I was sitting doing bookwork. I received a text from my cousin, Louise. She and her family lived in the little country town I grew up in. My aunty Tootie had been unwell for a while, and Louise had some news.

"Jo, Mum is in hospital. Are you able to come and visit her as she doesn't have much longer?"

"Oh no, Louise. Yes, of course."

I was devastated. I visited my aunty regularly over the years. She was the caring mother I never had. During our recent visits, I had been keeping her informed of Oscar's progress. She was a wonderful support for me. I loved her with all my heart.

I arrived at the small country hospital, parked the car and sat. I had been crying all the way and looked horrible, so I needed a little bit of time to compose myself. I got out of the car and walked across the long car park to the main entrance where I was directed to my aunt's room. Her family were there as well as my sisters. I walked up to her bed. She was so frail and her breathing was laboured. I took her hand and gave her a big hug and kiss. Having to say goodbye to this beautiful, caring woman pulled at my heart strings. I was crying. So much emotion was causing my body to shake.

Walking out of my aunt's hospital room with my sisters, I got upset as I remembered I hadn't told her that Oscar was going to be okay. *I have to go and tell her!*

The months of emotional fear tormented me, allowing my pain of loss to surface without resistance.

I lost the plot. I couldn't go back to my aunty because I was too emotionally distraught. It had been a big day. Feeling worn out and emotionally drained, I left to drive the 90 minutes home. My aunty passed away later that night. I was so grateful I was able to go and say goodbye to her.

September was the month for celebration. Oscar was in remission. My amazing, brave grandson had beaten this horrendous disease. There was still a long way to go, though. Kylie and Oscar couldn't come home for good yet.

Many weekends and odd days sitting with Oscar at the Brisbane townhouse were wonderful. He needed to exercise, so we would walk around the complex and play pool in the games room. One day, when I was visiting Oscar for the weekend, I asked him, "Is there anything you would love to do?'

"I want to kick a football and go to the beach."

"We can manage that."

The look on his face was priceless. We gathered up everything we needed, as Oscar was still taking a lot of medications. In the car, we sat looking at each other with huge grins on our faces. First stop: the shops. We bought a football and took off again towards the ocean. Along the way, we came across a large park. *Let's have some fun.* I parked the car. We got out and walked over to the open field. There weren't too many people milling around. Some were sitting, quietly enjoying their solitude, while others were throwing a ball through a basketball hoop.

> *So, we had a teenager who hadn't got all his strength back yet, and a 62-year-old grandma who doesn't run. Ever.*

Exceptions were made that day as I ran after many kicked footballs. Some dribbled just in front of Oscar, others he connected with, and in some instances, I had a way to run to bring the footy back. The decision I faced was: *do I try and kick the ball back to him? Or run it back? I can kick this football back to him. How hard could it be?* After numerous attempts of trying to connect with that damn football, I gave up and ran back to deliver the ball to Oscar. All the while he was laughing so hard, watching his grandma run around. I wasn't going to let Oscar know I was pooped, but luckily for me he said he was. We had a rest on the welcoming bench. Still laughing as we caught our breath.

Once we were breathing normally and had gulped down many slurps of water, we took off again, this time to find the beach. We came across a lovely area with a bench nestled under beautiful, shady trees. Many sea birds flew up and down, bombing the water, hoping to catch a meal. Oscar and I walked lazily along the shore, splashing water at each other. It was magical. Occasionally, we would find a bench and rest. After we had some lunch, we took off again, this time for the townhouse.

As we drove along, I asked Oscar, "Is there anything else you would like to do?'

"I would love an ice cream, Grandma."

"Done."

We found a Baskin-Robbins ice cream shop. Oscar chose a small tub of different flavours. It was a sweet ending to our beautiful day together. I will never forget the relaxed look on Oscar's face as he ate his ice cream. That look had been missing from my amazing grandson's face for too long.

In October 2017, Oscar was allowed to come home to the Sunshine Coast permanently. Archie went home to be with his mum, her partner and Oscar. Archie and I had over nine months together. There had been many emotional lows as well as many loving moments together. We helped each other get through an extremely tough year.

Archie was doing very well at school. His teacher and fellow students were asking many questions about his bone marrow transplant and how it all worked. After getting permission from his teacher, Archie and I put together a presentation to show the class. It went very well. Watching all the different expressions on Archie's friends' faces was heartwarming. Their care for Archie, and what he went through selflessly to help his big brother, was beautiful to witness.

Unbeknown to us, Archie's teacher had nominated Archie for the Fred Hollows Humanity Award.

This award recognises Year Six students who have made a positive difference in their community. It celebrates students who show compassion, integrity and kindness in their everyday lives.

In October, Archie, Oscar, Archie's teacher and I went to the awards ceremony at Parliament House in Brisbane. It was wonderful that Oscar was well enough to be there to support and celebrate his younger brother. I was astounded hearing all the students' amazing achievements to help their communities. I was extremely proud of Archie and so grateful to his teacher for nominating him.

Archie's school year was coming to an end. It had been a big year for him. Hannah had arrived from New South Wales. It was wonderful to see her when Oscar and I picked her up from the airport. It was a nice change to drive to Brisbane and not veer off to go to the townhouse or hospital.

While all of this was happening in my personal life, my professional life was on the downward trajectory. The business was financially screwed. No matter how hard I tried to convince my husband we had to change things, it still fell on deaf ears, which meant we were just digging a deeper hole for ourselves. Our marriage was suffering and I had thoughts of suicide, which frightened me. I knew what I was capable of. *Will this bloody business finally end me?*

I was seeing my counsellor regularly. Problems with the business and my financial situation overshadowed work I could have been doing to address the debilitating symptoms from my earlier abuses. The bloody business consumed my every waking moment. Binge eating, to try and bury my feelings, meant I was piling on the weight. I have intolerances to food containing gluten and lactose, yet all I wanted to do was eat all the foods that made me sick. Self-sabotage was working well.

I was very good at camouflaging my feelings. I wore many masks over the years, covering the agonising truth that lay below the surface. I was truly worried for my own wellbeing. Although I stayed strong for my family, never letting them see how destroyed I was, I was starting to feel that even their unconditional love would not be enough to stop me from falling into my familiar black hole. Each year that went past, I thought *surely, things cannot get any worse. Things must start to pick up now.* And each year, another horrendous disaster would engulf me.

Monthly visits to Brisbane for tests showed Oscar was still in remission. We were back to having sleepovers and spending precious time together.

Oscar said to me one day, "Grandma, if you hadn't pushed me to have blood tests done straight away after I was sick at the pool, my doctor told me I would have died. I was very sick."

I looked at him with tears in my eyes. "Sweetheart, you know I will do anything for you, right? If I can help it, I won't let anything happen to you. I love you so much."

Archie had started playing rugby on the Sunshine Coast. Taking him to training sessions and games helped take my mind off my financial predicament. I watched him play in the rain and in the howling wind. Whatever Mother Nature threw at us, we handled.

I was volunteering three days a week in the library at my grandkids' school. That was a great pacifier. Working with the adorable primary school students, who called me Grandma Jo, was the best medicine. Helping them chose their library books, making displays and being creative was so therapeutic for me. Unfortunately, some days my worries refused to part from me, leaving me emotional and fragile.

The librarian was a wonderful, caring and supportive lady. Her shoulder to cry on was my safe place on many occasions. A head teacher, who had her office in the library, was also a source of much love and understanding. Many wonderful, supportive lunches were had in the lunchroom alongside teachers, teacher aids, admin and other members of the school staff. I will never forget their kindness and support shown to me throughout Oscar's leukaemia journey as well as my own personal journey.

I was blessed to be in a caring environment where I knew I could be me, without judgement.

I was going to lose another home. Listing it for sale sent me into a combination of rage and denial. Self-hatred filled every cell of my being. *How did I allow this to happen again? I don't think I can do this again. I have no future. I am at the mercy of males no matter what I do or where I go. I have been screwed over once again.*

Our finances being what they were, I was advised to go on Newstart, then the disability pension. Because of my age and the fact that I already volunteered three days a week at the school, I didn't need to look for work, which I was very grateful for.

The house was on the market; we finally signed a contract that was to settle in November.

Oscar passed his learner's test, which meant another grandchild to teach how to drive. I loved it all over again, happy for the times spent with this amazing young man. He was making good progress with his health. Having missed so much of Year Ten, I would help Oscar with his assignments at home. Archie was doing well at school, enjoying his sport and being the lovable teenager, I adored.

My psychologist was doing everything she could to help me. On many occasions, I drove away from my home screaming, crying and wanting to end my miserable, pathetic life. I had spent too many years feeling this way. On top of all this, I was forced to ask family and friends for money to save the business. My self-esteem was buried under layers and layers of self-hatred.

Will this feeling of worthlessness ever end?

The stress of applying for house after house to rent also took its toll. With the house settlement date looming, I finally signed a lease. I was so thankful I had somewhere to live. I will probably never have my own home again as all the money from the house sale went towards paying off debts.

CHAPTER 15

Brave

Surviving trauma is to be brave, wipe away the tears
Don't close the door on your life, sweep away your fears
Allow light in to take away the dark
Find purpose in all that you do, ignite your inner spark
Love yourself and those who are dear to you
Happiness and peace are yours, it is true
You are safe

—Jo Wilcox

Blythe Baird, a well-known American poet and author on the topics of mental illness, eating disorders, sexuality, feminism and trauma, wrote, "To live in the body of a survivor is to never be able to leave the scene of the crime. I cannot ignore the fact that I live here."

I have lived tethered to the scene of my many traumas for over 60 years. I am tired. I don't want to fight anymore. I want to hang my head and allow the shadow of trauma to cloak me. To become lost and never found. The fire that constantly burns under my feet reminds me that if I give in to my ever-present symptoms of sexual abuse, all that will be left is a pile of ashes.

They say we can lose ourselves in a song, a beautiful day, a crossword, a drawing, a good book. Wonderful, feel-good activities. There is also a dark side to losing ourselves. Losing our self-identity, our self-love, our self-worth and our happiness leaves a soul broken and dissociated. Our personality fragments, allowing others to impose their will and idea of a good time on the unsuspecting victim. Days, months, years go by. As every day passes, there's a realisation that the likelihood of becoming whole again is lost. In its place is a broken woman, mostly void of happiness and peace.

Recovering from trauma is a full-time job. Almost every day, there is a test.

Australia's harsh environment, rapidly changing weather and distance from the rest of the world has produced a nation of strong, resilient and adaptable people. I am resilient, tenacious, strong and capable. I wouldn't have made it to being a senior citizen without being that way. But when my existence is overtaken by my DID characteristics, my ability to produce rational thought, comprehend what is playing out in my mind and carry on with my day is non-existent. There is nowhere else to go but follow the part's lead and succumb.

Trying to adapt to harsh and quickly changing conditions has crippled me. I may live in an amazing country, but I die over and over again when I am a captive of my fractured mind. To explain the many emotions that course through my body during an episode is difficult. Sometimes it is as quick as flicking a switch. An event can bring a part into my present surroundings without me being aware. The part will be feeling attacked or frightened by what transpired only moments before.

The memory that the part is protecting, and has hidden from me for years, is now front and centre. The tremendous pain and loss of control, which was experienced when it happened, is so vivid, so alive, that my part is feeling, smelling, hearing and seeing every aspect of the trauma as it unfolded many years ago. Because I feel what my part feels, all of these split-second emotions hit me like a cascade of bullets from a firing squad, causing my poor body to become confused and scared.

Of course, while all of this is happening, I am now a backseat passenger, relying completely on an unknown part of me calling the shots. I have no idea why I have become so animated. Scared, enraged and feeling so out of control. I don't know what has happened to trigger this. I can only surmise. Was it a loud noise? Was it a smell? Did someone walk past who reminded the part of a particular person? Did I see something on TV that disturbed my part? I am still trapped. First by my step-grandfather and now by the parts born from his abuse.

The aftermath of my dissociative episodes leaves me weakened, emotionally destroyed and vulnerable. My sun becomes less bright until my parts settle down and leave me in charge of my own existence once again. A dissociative episode is unpredictable – there is no warning.

It is definitely *not*: I will wake up tomorrow morning and schedule a dissociative episode.

It is definitely *not*: I will wake up tomorrow and remember everything I have done in my life.

It definitely *is* out of my control.

It definitely *is* going to be a part of me for the rest of my life.

Causes for my dissociation are many and varied. I have had many 'aha' moments along with some soul-destroying moments as I learnt more and more about myself, and my unpredictable and unbelievable life.

In my case, ignorance is not bliss. It is frightening.

In 2019, I was knocked back for the disability pension, which meant I had to gather more proof that I did indeed suffer from many forms of mental illness. The hoops I had to jump through did not help my sanity while I was trying to keep my business afloat as well. I was 64 and had another three years before I could go on the age pension.

2019 also saw me officially diagnosed with DID when I was referred to my second psychologist. My first psychologist strongly suspected I had DID, so she suggested I see a colleague who had trained and worked in the area of dissociation and trauma. Coping with depression, anxiety and confusion for most of my life I didn't feel that the abuses I had survived were relevant to my mental health. My emotional and sometimes disturbing journey delving into my DID experiences had begun.

This is what my psychologist witnessed at my first couple of sessions in March 2019:

"In Jo's first appointment, while she was very open about her history, she appeared visually cautious and wary. There was something a little different in the way she was checking me out, which is hard to describe but more of a feeling. When Jo seemed to present almost like a different person in the second session, gentler and softer in her personality, I realised I had met a different part of her in our initial session. When I reminded her of what we discussed in our first meeting, she had no memory of any of the content at all. Such is the nature of dissociation. From then on, I frequently wrote down and sent to Jo information or ideas that were important from our sessions so that she could go over it."

My life of confusion, shame and ignorance changed when I was diagnosed with DID. The diagnosis allowed me to understand my turbulent life and acknowledge the many parts of me born from child sexual abuse.

After a number of sessions, I wondered why my psychologist wasn't concerned if a part didn't have a name. She referred to them, for example, as 5-year-old part, or 13-year-old part. I asked her about parts having their own names. Her response was:

"If someone has a name for a part, that is okay. But I don't deliberately name parts because I don't want to increase the separation between parts of self-state. Parts of self-state do adapt and change. They have flexibility and so we want to allow for this in our identifying them. It is good to understand their age and function because we can know them if we meet them again. It is good to understand their function because then we can understand how and why they came into being and help them as a part of the person and as the whole person."

The initial list of parts I met back in 2000 (shared in Chapter 10) I named before seeing a psychologist. I have a number of different parts, and a few of these parts have presented more than once throughout my sessions. To make it easier for you to identify my parts, I decided to name them all. The names I chose are not used in my sessions. If a part has given my psychologist a name during a session, I have used that name they chose in my book.

I met a number of parts throughout my first year. The opening of Pandora's box left me having nightmares and daytime flashbacks. Having young parts cry uncontrollably during my sessions, because of the memories they were holding, was emotionally damaging for me. I was learning about traumas I had no idea had happened. One such memory, held by a young part I have named Charlotte, is about a wrought-iron bed.

What? I have no conscious recollection of a wrought-iron bed.

Charlotte cried and cried and was petrified throughout my whole session. She didn't talk. She just nodded or shook her head if she was asked a question. No information was given of that trauma.

How do I live with not knowing what happened on that wrought-iron bed? One day I might find out.

I had never felt this out of control, so horribly vulnerable.

I was taught to create a place in my mind where I could go to feel safe. My safe place was a wooden cabin in nature with a stream meandering past. I could hear the water flow steadily over the pebbles as I sat in my rocking chair on my porch. Animals, such as kangaroos, koalas, birds, even snakes, would approach me for a cuddle. There was no fear in my safe place. There were no people, either. Only the unconditional love of the animal kingdom to keep me company.

I could close my eyes and allow myself to be transported to my calm and safe place, where everything was magical.

I still go to my safe place when my life spirals out of control. Sometimes it works and I can calm down. Because work with my psychologist is ongoing, I still have new parts presenting themselves for help, causing me inner turmoil. My safe place isn't always enough to keep me stable.

I was having regular visits to my counsellor as well as taking part in group therapy. At one group session, a lady was very upset about her upcoming court date – she was another victim who had to prove beyond a reasonable doubt that she had been sexually abused. This lady touched my heart. I wanted to do something for her. I decided I would paint positive words on small flat rocks, along with a little poem and place them in a beautiful little drawstring bag to remind her that I was with her, if only in spirit, throughout her gruelling ordeal.

I thought about my life of abuse. *My step-grandfather is dead. I never told any professional people. I didn't go to the police so there is no proof, no police report number.* The court system is so archaic when it comes to any form of sexual abuse. Fortunately, there are organisations that lend support and knowledge to the survivor, helping with paperwork that may be needed to prove the abuse occurred. They can also accompany them to court sessions, so the survivor always feels supported and encouraged to tell their truth.

There are also professionally trained court assistance dogs. Their job is to provide emotional support and comfort to people while they navigate the unrelenting justice system. These amazing animals provide a healthy, calming distraction from an overwhelming trauma response.

I would have liked to take my abuser to court and see him punished. The need for retribution weighed heavily on me. *I will never have closure. I suppose my closure is that he is dead and he cannot hurt me anymore. I just need to have my parts realise that fact also. Easier said than done sometimes.*

No one knows someone else's backstory. The reasons that stop a victim from reporting their abuse are numerous and varied. I have several reasons for not reporting my abuse. I was only a child, and my generation didn't think child abuse was an issue. I was threatened with: "If you tell anyone, I will hurt your younger sisters." The fear of getting in trouble if I told – because it would have been my fault – stopped me from ever telling any adults or professionals about my child sexual abuse.

Our past definitely drives our present.

Attitudes are changing about the impact abuse of any kind has on a victim, although many societal beliefs are still cemented in the ice age. One day the ice will melt and every child's safety will be paramount, rather than the fear of rocking the boat. Similarly, I would like to think the attitude towards violence against women will change for the better in the not-too-distant future.

For many years, I have helped myself through natural therapies. I have been seeing my chiropractor for 10 years. I know when my spine is out of alignment because it puts pressure on my nervous system. My anxiety, and fight, flight, freeze and fawn responses, are worse than normal. I also have pain. He also uses kinesiology to ask the body what areas need to be worked on, and Neuro Emotional Technique (NET).

Doing an NET session before I leave, also helps me with my stuck emotional patterns, which have manifested from fear, grief and many other negative emotions. If I do not let go of these emotions, they can cause adverse reactions in my body, like self-sabotage behaviours, destructive beliefs, phobias as well as chronic physical problems. I always feel so much better after the sessions with my chiropractor. I have found something that helps.

Over the years, I have also tried meditation, energy healing, acupuncture, reiki, tapping, hypnotherapy, naturopathy, hydrotherapy, herbal medicine, homeopathy and massage. I have tried to improve the environment around me by introducing feng shui. I have seen improvements with all of them. Trauma is fluid – it ebbs and flows. Everyone deals with it differently.

My counsellor helped me send an application to Victim Assist Queensland (VAQ), which provides financial assistance for victims of violent crime. VAQ also helps victims understand their rights and where they can go to get the support they may need.

My counsellor was hoping that if I could supply proof of my various treatments, I may receive some financial reimbursement from VAQ. It took me months to gather documents from all the relevant places, including medical professionals, therapists and information from my own diaries going back as many years as I could.

Unfortunately, because my abuse was historical, meaning it happened many years ago, there wasn't any police report and my abuser was dead, therefore my application was knocked back. Even though it was a refusal, I received a beautifully worded email from VAQ, and I was touched by the kindness and understanding that flowed from it. I was disappointed, but I understood their reasons.

It is our right as human beings to receive help and understanding.

Being very honest, I felt like I didn't matter. I was again rejected, left to fend for myself. I didn't have the benefit of frequent sessions as I don't meet the criteria to receive funding through either Victims of Crime, the National Redress Scheme or the NDIS.

I had fallen through all these cracks. Even though I had been sexually abused for many years of my childhood as well as during my adulthood by more than one perpetrator, I had no proof. Other significant adverse life events have also added to my mental health issues.

If only I had told my secret, would it have made a difference? I didn't know about any of the organisations that help the victims of heinous sexual crimes.

Discovering 30-year-old Wicked Wendy answered a question that had always bothered me: why had my father called me a slut? This is when I was introduced formally to the part who was the cause of my father's embarrassment.

Wicked Wendy survived on intimate physical touch. She was not at all worried about where she found her male companionship. As long as her desires for sexual connection were met, she was satisfied. My understanding of what happened back in the 1980s wasn't brought to my attention until 2020. My psychologist's explanation said it all.

Because the sexual abuse had lasted a number of years, I became addicted to the abuse. As I got older, I craved control, something that has always been lacking in my life. Wicked Wendy was born to secretly satisfy that craving through sex. Her behaviour never considered that I had two children who needed me to be there for them – to nurture and protect them. She was the instigator, the dominatrix. There were no inhibitions when Wicky Wendy went out to play. She made sure no one told her what to do and how to do it. She had complete control over what could be done to her body.

I do not know what Wicked Wendy got up to during her escapades. I totally dissociated, I lost time, I do not remember people Wicked Wendy may have had sex with. I was not present when she was out and about. I had an answer to why I had an unknown man visit my home late one night.

I realise now that my father may have seen me during one of Wicked Wendy's liaisons. If this was the case, I do not blame him for the response he had. My father is dead now. However, if he was still alive, I would apologise to him for what Wicked Wendy did so many years ago. I would try and explain my DID. I would tell him that I loved him.

During this time in the 80s I was at my darkest, as far as my dissociations were concerned. I hadn't yet been diagnosed. My mind whirled around like a boomerang being thrown high into the air. Once thrown, a boomerang has the ability to return on its own. A marvellous Indigenous Australian feat. Will my memory ever return to me like the trustworthy boomerang?

The different parts that I am meeting have helped me realise why, over the years, I have had numerous bouts of losing control. My confusion and utter helplessness sometimes resulted in self-harm. I would either stab myself in my arm or stomach with a knife, scissors or nail file, bang my head against the wall until I had a whopper of a bump and later a bruise, or scratch my arms or my face with my own fingernails until I bled. Whatever was closest when I lost the plot was my weapon of choice.

What do I say if someone asks me about my wounds? I became a master of excuses. I didn't like telling untruths to my family and friends, but it was for their wellbeing.

"Oh, I scratched myself while I was cutting down the trees."

"I wasn't watching where I was going, and I tripped and bumped my head."

These were plausible excuses as I had a big yard, which needed constant pruning and weeding, and everyone trips over. I had this covered.

During another of my psychology sessions, Olivia, a 27-year-old part, emerged. Olivia held the memory of the horrendous night before my first wedding, which spilled over to the embarrassment of my wedding day. An unimaginable grief enveloped every word that Olivia said. Feeling like no one loved her kept her sobbing uncontrollably. Grieving for the love and respect she knew she had lost.

In 2020, it had been over 40 years since that miserable day. Feeling this part's raw emotions was overwhelming for me. I had no conscious idea that I had been grieving for a wedding day that could have been the happiest day of my life. I felt betrayed by both my father and my first husband. Neither man has any idea how devastated and irreparably hurt I was during that distressing time.

CHAPTER 16

Stops and starts

They run, they jump, they lick your face
Your warm lap is their happy place
They are your comfort when you are sad
Their mischievous antics sometimes make you mad
Our amazing pets help us to laugh and live
Unconditional love every day is what they give
I love you

—Jo Wilcox

Oscar still had monthly visits back to Lady Cilento Children's Hospital in Brisbane. Either Kylie or I would take him down. Something had been troubling me ever since Oscar was diagnosed with leukaemia. I had the opportunity to talk to him one day as we sat waiting to see a doctor.

"Oscar, I want to apologise to you."

"What for, Grandma? What would you have done that you have to apologise to me for?"

"When I would come and pick you up for school before you were diagnosed, you were not ready. I would have to hurry you along to get dressed and get your stuff together for school. I realise now that you weren't ready because you were sick. You were tired from having leukaemia for so long and we didn't know. I am so sorry I got impatient with you so many times." I tried so hard not to cry, but my guilt associated with this realisation had been weighing on my heart for a long time.

With tears in his eyes, Oscar gave me a big hug and said, "Grandma, you don't have to apologise. I understand. I love you."

With Oscar missing Year Ten, we had talks with his teacher, who was hoping to make the rest of his educational journey a little bit easier. A suggestion was made that Oscar could participate in a school-based traineeship, which typically takes two to four years. Oscar was happy to do that, so Oscar and I decided he would do his traineeship with me.

Doing the traineeship would get Oscar through his secondary education with as little fuss and worry as possible. Meetings with the teacher and Oscar's traineeship organisation manager saw him kick off his Certificate III in Warehousing.

In the first half of 2019, we were summoned to a meeting by our franchisor business manager. *What could this be all about?* At this stage, we had been with this franchisor for 21 years. We were hit with a bombshell. We were not wanted anymore. Restructuring their franchise model, they only wanted one distributor on the Sunshine Coast. This resulted in us being discarded like a piece of rotten meat on 31 December 2019. Our business was unsaleable as the franchise agreement only had several months remaining. We had employees who would lose their jobs and we had trucks we were still paying off. *How will Oscar finish his certificate? Shit, shit, shit.*

Big business, big bucks. We were screwed. They knew it and didn't give a shit.

My depression had taken hold of me. Emotions so negative clouded my thoughts and diminished my ability to see anything but failure and disappointment as my legacy. I cried. I talked shit to myself, blaming, punishing and putting myself down. I pulled at my hair. I walked around aimlessly, wanting to end my madness. I started sweating while my heart beat out of rhythm in my chest. The hurt was so overwhelming. All I could think was *I want the hurt to stop. I just want it to stop*. In other words: *I want to die. I just want to die.*

We were given the option of leaving immediately or toughing out the last few months of our business life. We decided to stay and pay off as much debt as we could. Both my husband and I were devastated beyond comprehension. *Things couldn't possibly get any worse.*

I had a meeting with my employees to let them know they would be out of a job at the end of the year. My anxiety was through the roof.

I didn't have butterflies in my tummy – I had bull elephants stomping around heavily. *No one should have to go through this just because of someone's greedy business decision.*

"It is your choice to stay until the end of the year or leave now. I support whatever you decide."

Each employee took a couple of days to make their decision. I was overwhelmed when I was told by each one that they would see the year out with my husband and me. Some of my employees had been with us for over 15 years. They were family – an amazing, loyal bunch of people.

The pressure was on for both Oscar and me to finish up his traineeship. Thankfully, we got it done successfully. Oscar was the proud owner of a Certificate III in Warehousing. Woohoo. Oscar's bravery and tenacity shone through once again. I was so proud of him.

I still volunteered in the school library and, for a short while, in the school canteen. My years volunteering at the school were very happy. Another little job at the school entailed helping a wonderful little boy with autism. I was very honoured to be chosen as this little boy's companion. I would help him transition from his mum to the classroom each morning. He was a treasure. Once we got to know each other, my mothering instinct and my gut feelings helped me navigate this sometimes very stressful time with love and understanding. As the years went on, I was no longer needed as this amazing little man was able to complete his daily school routine with ease. It was my pleasure to be part of this young boy's life, if only for a short while.

Oscar was racking up his driving hours. Eventually, the day came for his driving test. There were nerves all around as Oscar went off with the test instructor and I waited patiently for him to return. He passed. I was so proud.

November saw Oscar graduate from Year Twelve, with Archie finishing Year Eight the following month. Hannah came up from New South Wales to attend Oscar's formal with the rest of the family. The students in Year Twelve had been practising dance moves in preparation for their formal. I had a tear in my eye as I watched Oscar walk across the dance floor to ask his mum to dance. It warmed my heart to see my amazing daughter and my just as amazing grandson twirl around the dance floor together. I was a very proud lady that night.

The pressure of knowing I would have to walk away from the business in a few short months was horrendous. There would be no financial renumeration – just pack up my things and leave. I blamed myself for everything that was happening to our business. *If only I had the courage years ago to stand up. If only I wasn't such a wimp. If only. If only.*

If you are told enough times, "You are worthless," or words to that effect, you will start to believe it. It becomes your truth. Just like a sexual predator grooms his prey, leaving them with self-loathing as their barometer, a person who uses words to control another will leave an indelible mark on them.

During a session, I asked my psychologist, "Why do I always blame myself?"

She replied, "Why do people blame themselves? Illusion of control. For example, I am stupid or unworthy, or it is my fault. If we do this, then it gives us the illusion of control. It is better to think this than to think we are totally powerless. Or another way to look at it is: if we think it is our fault and our caregivers are good, that is better than thinking our caregivers are dangerous. This would leave us in a more vulnerable position."

We downsized from two cars to one and sold everything that wasn't nailed down. We needed every bit of cash we could lay our hands on. Needless to say, Christmas 2019 wasn't very happy.

I had advertised our trucks on Truck Sales and anywhere else I could. It would make no difference what I tried to do to get the trucks sold. The COVID-19 pandemic was upon us, businesses were closing down, no one was buying trucks. We were rightly screwed. The banks who held the loans on our trucks were on my back, wanting the payments met. An impossibility.

Standing in my own darkness,
tears of despair slowly escaped
from my eyes. I was crushed.

COVID lockdowns were continuous, leaving me unable to see Oscar or Archie, or volunteer at the school.

My health was becoming worse. My blood pressure was way too high, causing me to have dizzy spells, which led to panic attacks and horrendous sleeping patterns. Heart palpitations, confusion and loss of concentration didn't help me navigate the enormous mountain of bookwork I had to do every day whether I felt like it or not. Phone calls and emails were the bane of my existence, causing headaches that took hours from my day.

Some of my parts are not holders of traumatic memories. On the contrary, they are helpers in my everyday life. Competent Cate, a 27-year-old part that I identified early on, has been my mainstay. She helped me negotiate my divorce and manoeuvre my way through all of my business escapades. Her tenacity and fearless attitude deserve a medal along with my humble gratitude.

My anger management was non-existent, leaving Miss Angry to cause a ruckus, while my fight, flight, freeze or fawn responses were heightened. Many days of not leaving the house, not showering, not changing my clothes and not brushing my teeth only darkened my mood.

I needed help. Doing something I had never done before, I rang Beyond Blue. I spoke to a very caring person for some time.

That phone call saved my life that day.

I need to use this resource more often. It was a bright light while going down my tunnel of dread and despair.

Around the same time, Centrelink approved my application for the disability pension with the help of Narelle from Capa Services. They are a national company based in North Lakes, Queensland. I was so relieved. *I will have money to live for a little while longer.*

My happy place was my dog Silver. I loved him with all my heart. He was so loyal, obedient and loving. He would go running and walking with me. He was amazing with my grandchildren. So gentle and patient. Silver always knew when I wasn't doing very well because he would intuitively want to be close to me.

One morning, I went outside to hang the washing on the line. "Hello, my beautiful boy." I could see there was something wrong as Silver struggled to make it to his feet. I ran over to him and looked into his eyes. They weren't right.

"There is something wrong with Silver!" I yelled to my husband.

He came out and agreed with me.

"Call the vet. I will take him straight there now."

I was holding back tears. I was so scared. My husband and I carefully lifted Silver into the back of my car. The trip to the vet was dreadful. I started to cry. My gut was telling me my gorgeous boy was very unwell.

Pulling up at the vet's, I rang to let them know I was parked out the back. The lady came out to the car and did some tests on him as he lay motionless with laboured breathing.

"Will he be okay?" I sputtered between sniffles.

"I feel he has cancer."

How could she know that?

"What? He cannot have cancer. He hasn't been sick. He is still eating."

I was now full-blown howling. *This is not happening. I cannot lose my best friend.*

I looked at her with pleading eyes. "You can fix him, right?'

"He is very sick. I feel the cancer is through his body. The humane thing to do is put him to sleep."

Crying uncontrollably, I couldn't believe what I was hearing.

"You stay here with Silver. Take as long as you like to say goodbye to him. When you are ready, come in and let me know."

I was distraught. My world was falling apart. My beautiful boy was going to leave me. I sat in the back of the car, holding him for a long time.

"I love you, Silver. I don't want you to go. Please don't leave me."

I cradled his head as I felt the life drain out of him. I squeezed him even tighter as his eyes closed and he stopped breathing. My best mate had just passed away in my arms.

How could Silver be this sick and me not know?

I sat with him, in disbelief, my tears coming to rest on his fur. It seemed like an eternity before I had the strength to leave him and walk inside and tell the lady he had passed away.

I asked her, "How did I not know he was sick?"

"Some dogs with cancer do not show any symptoms until the dog all of a sudden becomes extremely ill. There was nothing you could have done for Silver."

He was 15 years old. Guilt swept through my body. I didn't have the money to have Silver cremated so I could keep him with me forever. I couldn't take my best friend home. I couldn't bear to leave him, but I had to. His collar was all I had left of my loving, beautiful boy. The vet's bill for Silver's next step was put on my almost-maxed-out credit card. I was inconsolable. *You useless piece of shit. You have no money. How could you just leave him there, alone? He is special and needs to be treated with love and respect. You cannot do anything right.*

Covid started to slow its roll. Oscar and Archie were a constant in my life once again. Every weekend they would visit to work on Oscar's Civic, lovingly called "Ronda the red-hot Honda". I helped a lot. I moved stuff, picked up stuff, put down stuff, held on to stuff, washed stuff. I was the best/worst help they could have. We laughed a lot as I asked what the grandboys thought were crazy questions. I did actually learn a lot about cars and how to fix them though.

I would be inside, doing my own thing, when I would hear:

"Grandma, we need your help."

"Okay. What do I have to do?'

"Stand here and hold this."

So, I would hold *this* – whatever "this" was at the time.

I also calmed down these two loving brothers if a project, like wrapping the car, was causing endless frustration. *Just say something silly, Jo. That will help them take a breath and start again.* Fun times. I loved every moment of every day they spent with me.

I was able to recommence volunteering at the school. Everyone was finally seeing some normality come back into their life.

Oscar rang. “Grandma, would you help me do up my resume for a job I saw? It is for an apprentice mechanic at Sunshine Toyota in their customer service workshop at Sippy Downs.”

“Of course, sweetheart. Come on up and we will get it done.”

A couple of months went past. I received a phone call from Sunshine Toyota, asking me about Oscar’s school-based traineeship, his work ethic, and so on. Of course, my responses were extremely positive. *I wonder if this man knows I am also Oscar’s grandma.*

A few days later, I got a phone call from Oscar.

“Grandma, guess what?”

“What, sweetheart?”

“I got the job!”

“Woohoo! How wonderful. Congratulations.”

“Thank you so much, Grandma, for helping me. I couldn’t have done this without you.”

We hung up and I did a happy dance. *It is about time Oscar had his dreams come true.*

My life is held together by the continuous love I feel from my family.

With Oscar working full-time, I was back driving Archie places. We had sold one of our trucks, which was a blessing. I had also approached the banks we owed money to, asking if they would forgive the remaining debts. No.

One afternoon, I was walking along the footpath, heading to the supermarket to buy my groceries, when I encountered a man walking in front of me. He was on his phone, not really watching where he was going. My fear was that he would turn into a shop unexpectedly and I would run into him. The thought of having an unknown male touch me, especially if I wasn't prepared for it, was absolutely horrifying.

So, I kept my distance behind him. My instincts were correct. Next minute, he turned abruptly for the coffee shop, still immersed in his phone. *Shit.* There was enough space between us to avoid a collision. As I walked past him, I let out a sigh of relief and I said quietly, "I am safe." Well, my words mustn't have been quiet enough as he thought I was abusing him for being on his phone.

What happened next was totally out of my control. I turned and faced him. I could feel the anger well up in me, but I still felt anxious. I could also feel that this wasn't me. This all happened in a split second. *Crap – my angry part.* The one who protects me was out and about. She wasn't going to have this. There were other people around, but that made no difference. Next minute, Miss Angry was letting this guy have it.

"Excuse me, I was sexually abused as a small child. To protect myself, I stayed behind you until I felt it was safe for me to go past. I didn't want to bump into you. I couldn't care less that you were on your phone."

His reaction was unexpected.

"I am so sorry you had those things happen to you. I am sorry."

I smiled and walked away. *Oh, my goodness.* I was shaking like a leaf. I had to sit down, so I went to the toilet.

I stayed there until I felt whole again. Funny way of putting it, I know. But that is how it is.

DID at its best. When I dissociate, without consciously knowing I have, it is a real problem. That rarely happens now because of the EMDR work I am doing with my psychologist. My parts are starting to understand that we are now an adult, that we are safe. It has taken a long time to get to where I am today.

The parts that do speak up at my sessions do not always tell us about the memories they are holding on to. Often, they are too distraught to speak. There will be a part or parts that hold various memories. They may have visited one of my sessions, or they may not have yet. No part is pushed for information because, in reality, it is *me* who is being pressured to relive memories that are just too painful. I need to be able to leave my sessions in a manageable state of mind, rather than being too deeply triggered.

At one point, I stopped seeing my psychologist for about six months. Every time I had an upcoming appointment, I would have horrific nightmares, followed by long bouts of not sleeping at all. It was like all my parts were making sure I didn't have the energy or inclination to disturb the status quo. I couldn't handle seeing my psychologist while dealing with my everyday life. I needed to have a break, to gather my strength, to be able to start the healing process again. I felt it was the best decision for me at the time, but I knew I couldn't ignore my trauma forever.

CHAPTER 17

Family

Wonderful times, happy times
Overwhelming times, soul-destroying times
Laughter will ring out, tears will be shed
Hugs and kisses will be shared with love
Holding hands, helping each other up
Showing vulnerability, allowing help to comfort you
Being part of a family encompasses all of this and more

—Jo Wilcox

Archie was 16 years old and, by gaining his learner's permit, had put me back in the driver supervisor role. He was learning to drive Oscar's manual car. I have a manual licence but hadn't driven a manual for years and years. Archie would drive my automatic car to school, rugby training and anywhere else he or I needed to go. Oscar had his car at work, so we had the use of it when he finished work and on the weekends. This is when Archie, Oscar and I went driving.

Oscar's tall frame would squish into the back seat of his two-door Holden Barina, while I sat in the passenger seat with heaps of room for my short legs. The supervisor has to sit in the front. Otherwise, I would have let Oscar sit there. In between bites of snacks, Oscar would instruct Archie on when to change gears. There was some kangaroo hopping as well as some stalling, but eventually Archie mastered the gear stick and away we would go.

Oscar was so caring and selfless. Not many young men would give up so much of their spare time to help their little brother learn to drive. We had so much fun. I watched Archie's eyes dart from windscreen to tachometer, following Oscar's instructions to the tee, as he navigated corners, stop signs, hill starts and traffic lights. Memories I will never forget.

Seeing as Oscar had his Ps and Archie had his Ls, we decided to take a road trip down to see Hannah in New South Wales, a 14-hour drive. The grandboys and I had a wonderful trip, laughing, singing, chatting and enjoying each other's company.

Our time with Hannah was wonderful – it was so great to spend time with her. We went sightseeing, enjoying the Taronga Western Plains Zoo and a motor car museum. I felt so blessed to have my three loving grandchildren around me again.

Month after month went past. I was running out of steam, walking around in a terrified daze most of the time. The overwhelming worry around the debt we owed the banks had awakened the trauma caused by the first time we lost everything. My stress levels were high all the time, sometimes feeling unmanageable. *I don't know if I can do this anymore.*

One time, I was having an extremely distressing episode, and I needed to be on my own. I drove to the botanical gardens. In the car park, there were between 30 and 40 spare car bays. I parked one car bay away from the very end, where the bushland started. I put up the windscreen sunshade, so no one could see me. I always made sure I could see anyone coming near me as well.

I was going to put my fold-up chair in the one spare car bay facing the bush. I was just about to open my car door and get my chair out of the back when a man in a large utility swung into the car bay between me and the bush.

Why? There are so many other car bays. Why are you parked next to me? I was destroyed. Within seconds I was shaking uncontrollably. My fear barometer had just burst. All I could think was: *the only reason he would park here is so he can hurt me.* I couldn't console myself. I frantically tried to take down the sunshade and get the bloody key in the ignition. My hand was shaking so badly I felt I would never be able to get away.

I am trapped. I am done for. The car finally started. I didn't even look – I backed out of the car bay so fast that I almost ended up in the bush behind me. I sped off, screaming. My heart was pounding. I thought I was going to throw up. I felt so vulnerable.

Terrified tears rolled down my cheeks like a waterfall cascading over an impenetrable mountaintop.

I was constantly wiping my eyes, trying to help my blurred vision. I drove around for a long time, not remembering where I had been and not knowing where I was going. *I can't stop driving. He is following me. He will get me if I stop.*

The traumas from my past were screwing with my head. Parts that were holding memories of being attacked had taken control. I had no pictures filling my head – just the traumatic response to whatever had transpired so many years ago. *I better pull up in case a part does come out totally. I don't want to crash and maybe hurt someone else.*

I pulled up on the side of the road, turned off the ignition and tried to take myself to my happy place. *You can do it. Breathe, breathe.* I started to see my little wooden cabin, my rocking chair and the meandering stream, settling down as each piece of my happy place came into view in my mind. It took over half an hour for me to feel that I could drive again. I had stopped crying only to feel totally exhausted. I didn't want to go home, so I kept driving around for a while.

No one deserves to have this debilitating reaction take over their existence, demanding total servitude, all because of a man who died in 1977.

It was a prerequisite of the banks that I keep them updated regarding our financial circumstances. During one of these phone calls, I was asked, “Do you have a financial adviser who can help you?”

“No, I don’t.”

This man was extremely helpful and understanding. In order for him to help me with the truck debt, he needed me to make an appointment with a financial adviser.

“The Salvation Army has a financial assistance counselling service. Give them a call and make an appointment, and then get back to me,” he instructed.

“Okay. I will.”

He proceeded to give me the number for the Salvation Army Moneycare Counselling Service. I rang and made an appointment and then rang him back with the information he requested. I had never heard of this service before. It is a free service for people with financial difficulties.

Desperation had walked with me for a while now. The loss of hope piggybacked on my feeling of being trapped with no way out. The chain of events up to this point clouded my judgement, leaving me wondering if I had made the right decision not declaring bankruptcy. Any dreams and goals I may have had over the years were just faded memories.

I hope with all my heart that this person can help me.

Waking to the sound of the parrots feeding from the bottlebrush outside my window always made me feel that it was going to be a good day.

Oscar was enjoying his job and Archie was happily racking up driving hours. My emotional wellbeing was still very volatile, causing each day to be an unknown quantity. My stressful life sought to drag me down into my second home, my black hole, which was the exact opposite of my mind's happy place. I wished on many occasions that my happy place was real – that I could leave all my traumatic memories outside my front gate, living with peace and quiet for the rest of my days.

I had just got home from running errands when my mobile rang. It was Hannah.

"Hello, sweetheart."

"Hello, Grandma. How are you going?"

"I am good, sweetheart. How are things going with you?'

"Grandma, I am pregnant."

"What? Oh, my goodness! What? How are you feeling? When are you due? Are you feeling, okay?"

"I am due around late May, early June, Grandma."

My beautiful granddaughter is having a baby. What am I going to be called?

Hannah had been living in New South Wales since 2017. She had met a wonderful young man called Marc. They had been together for a couple of years. Hannah went off the pill, thinking it would be a while before she fell pregnant. How wrong she was. A precious little surprise was going to bless my growing family.

I was floating on a cloud. It was September 2022. By June the following year, I would have a great grandbaby. My good day intuition was spot on. I was walking around the house with a big smile. I happily wandered into the lounge room and told my husband he was going to be a great-grandad. He was so happy. It was wonderful for us to have something positive to look forward to.

A couple of months later, I received dreadful news from my dear friend, Lyn. Roy had beaten his cancer and was in remission until a few months earlier. Unexpectedly, his lymphoma had returned. The cancer was so aggressive it was only a short time before he was admitted to palliative care. I visited them both, chatting about anything and everything. Roy was getting tired, so I said my goodbyes with a big hug and a loving kiss for my wonderfully caring and supportive friend.

A couple of days later, Roy passed away. Some doctors say if a cancer patient remains in complete remission for five years, they are most likely cured. My dear friend was diagnosed in 2017 and passed away in 2022.

Cancer is a deadly mistress, toying with its host, allowing a false sense of control over their own health.

My high blood pressure had returned. Medication wasn't the answer. My hypersensitivity saw to that. The ultimate solution, of course, would be to minimise stress in my life.

I had returned to my psychologist once more. In one session another young girl presented. I named her Amy. Her fear and vulnerability while she was a child were too much for her to contain. I had been having horrendous nightmares and these were because of Amy. I was very fragile mentally. *Something has to change for me to survive this.*

By the end of January 2023, the bank debts had been waived and the business was deregistered. Those three years were gruelling, to say the least. Seeking professional help from the Salvation Army's Moneycare representative was my saving grace. With the added support of my professional health team, I am hoping my journey will be a little easier to navigate as time goes on.

I am now a stronger person, making my own decisions as far as my personal financial future is concerned.

Archie celebrated his 17th birthday. We had made an appointment for his manual driving test. With Oscar's help, Archie was now proficient handling a manual car. The day of the test arrived, and Archie was good to go. The all-too-familiar sitting around, waiting for him to return from the test, was agonising. This was my third time as supervisor and I was still nervous. David's job as driving lesson teacher had also come to an end for my family. He has been a wonderful guide through the process of watching Hannah, Oscar and Archie gain their independence.

I watched as Archie and the test instructor stepped out of the car and walked towards the office. Then the driving test instructor turned and said with a smile, "You passed, Archie."

I was ecstatic with relief.

"How wonderful! Congratulations, sweetheart. I am so proud of you." The words just tumbled out of my mouth before anyone else could utter a word. I was beaming and had to contain myself, so I didn't break into a happy dance.

"Grandma, you are more excited than I am," Archie said with a big grin on his face.

"I know, sweetheart."

It was 2015 when I first became a learner driver supervisor for Hannah. I was 60 years old then. I had been so worried that I would be too old to teach Archie to drive when the time came. At 68 years old, I blitzed it. And just like that, my supervising role had come to an end.

Meanwhile, Hannah was busily getting everything prepared for her baby shower. I didn't go. I was exhausted and my financial situation didn't allow it. I was extremely upset that I wasn't going. A wonderful time was had by all, with many photos taken so I could feel part of it when everyone returned home. Hannah and I stayed in close contact as the delivery date came closer.

A wonderful Mother's Day, spent with Kylie, Oscar and Archie, came and went. The grandboys were busy with everything cars at my place each weekend. They would take me out to lunch, buy me beautiful things and just love me unconditionally. I was the most blessed grandma in the world.

The big day arrived at the beginning of June 2023 when I became a great-grandma to a little girl named Ivy. Oh, my goodness. Words couldn't express the absolute love I had for my family at that time. All was right in my world.

Kylie's excitement at being a grandma was wonderful to witness. She invited me to travel down to New South Wales to meet Ivy. We left at 4am and drove straight through, arriving at our destination at 5:30pm.

"Hello, Ivy. I am your great-grandma. I love you so much."

We talked about what Ivy was going to call me. We settled on sticking with Grandma even though she was a new generation. It just felt right. We had many wonderful visits with Hannah, Marc and Ivy. So many loving cuddles. It was heart-wrenching to say goodbye and make the long trip back to the Sunshine Coast.

I had a couple of days away, visiting my younger sister Lisa and her daughter, Katherine. I was sitting at the table, having a cuppa, before heading back home.

"Jo, have you got all your stuff?" Lisa called from the other room.

I could feel a familiar sensation wash over me. My eyes were staring at the floor as my head hung down. Lisa was talking to me, asking me to do something for her. *Why is she whispering? Why are my eyes all funny?* After a couple of minutes, I could lift my head and hear what was going on around me. I was really scared. I was not aware of this happening to me outside of a safe environment. *Did I just dissociate again? Oh, shit. Is this going to happen anywhere now?*

I do not remember what may have happened to bring on this dissociative episode.

"Jo, did you hear me? Is everything okay?"

"Yes, all good. I have got everything."

At my next psychologist appointment, I was too embarrassed to tell her about this episode. I was in denial that I had DID. *I am not this person. I am normal.*

2023 would be Archie's last year of schooling on the Sunshine Coast before he planned to head off to Brisbane to attend Queensland University of Technology (QUT). Archie and his dad attended the QUT Open Day, asking many questions and gathering a lot of information. Over the next few months, Archie and I would sit together in front of his laptop, perusing the QUT website, discussing the subjects he would take and when they were available.

Kylie was also busy helping Archie prepare for his formal. Fittings for his suit were well underway. He also needed photos of his pre-school year for the end-of-year celebrations, so we eagerly looked through the many photos I had on my laptop, coming across wonderful memories from the past. The grandboys were my constant sidekicks. It didn't matter what we got up to. Sharing each other's company was all we needed.

Oscar was enjoying his job and started attending TAFE courses in Brisbane. Archie was driving himself to school and his casual job. My grandbabies had all grown up.

The boys had been doing a lot of work on Ronda the red-hot Honda, getting her ready for sale. Oscar had a buyer, so he came to my place to put the finishing touches on his car and waited for the man to arrive. Ronda was sold and taken away on a trailer. Oscar started to sell off car parts and equipment he no longer needed. Many weekends spent together, watching movies, or playing cards or board games, made my life bearable.

"Grandma, what do you want to watch today – the Chrises or Liam?"

"Let's go with the Chrises today."

I have this little grandma crush on Chris Hemsworth, Chris Pratt and Chris Evans. Oscar and Archie thought it was hilarious. I would get lovingly teased about it all the time.

Worryingly, Oscar had been having headaches in the last few months.

"Grandma, do you have Panadol? I have a headache."

"Sure, sweetheart. I will get you some."

I got Oscar a couple of Panadol tablets and a glass of water. *I wonder if he is drinking enough water.*

When Oscar had leukaemia, it was a constant struggle to keep him hydrated. The chemotherapy treatments dried out his system. Surgery, radiation and some medications were also culprits. If he got too dehydrated, he would have headaches, which interfered with his healing. Sometimes, he would have to go back into hospital and be put on an intravenous drip.

"Here you go, Oscar. Are you drinking enough water, sweetheart? You might be dehydrated."

"Probably not, Grandma. You know what I am like." We both grinned at each other as I gave Oscar a second glass of water to drink.

CHAPTER 18

Challenges

Will I buckle under the pressure?
Will I hang my head and give in?
The road ahead has many twists and turns
Will I stay focused and brave?
Will I succumb and drop into my black hole?
Will I rise to the challenge and push through?
Will I love myself enough to keep going?
I will endure, I will help my family endure
The passing of time will soften the suffering
With courage I will survive
With love I will hold dear those who have been by my side
With perseverance I will face my challenges head on
Staying strong to open my heart and share my love

—Jo Wilcox

Hannah, Marc and Ivy were up from New South Wales, holidaying on the Gold Coast. Oscar and Archie were excited to holiday with their sister and her lovely family. On Friday, the 1st of September, Oscar suffered a terrible migraine at work. Not wanting to miss seeing his family, Oscar decided to go to his dad's on Saturday with Archie. Unfortunately, the migraine and vomiting didn't subside, and Oscar was in horrendous, persistent pain. On Sunday, Brett decided to take Oscar to the Royal Brisbane and Women's Hospital. Many tests later, Oscar was diagnosed with a brain bleed.

Archie came home on Sunday as he had his Year Twelve exams that week. He was devastated and worried about Oscar. Visiting me each day after he finished his exams, we chatted and supported each other as best we could. Kylie was beside herself with worry as she went down to be with Oscar. I am sure she was thinking how she would manage to stay strong for Oscar as he navigated another extremely serious health issue.

I can only imagine what was going through Oscar's mind. I am sure he was devastated, bewildered and scared. He knew what was ahead of him, having already been through a major health challenge. The diagnosis explained why Oscar had been having headaches for a while.

The "if only" scenarios started to pile up in my mind. "If only I had suggested he see a doctor." "If only I had asked Oscar how he was feeling." "If only I had taken more notice." I was beating myself up big time.

Kylie explained to me that he would have a brain biopsy in the next week or so, but they didn't know what day. I texted Oscar every day to tell him I loved him.

The agony of not being able to see Oscar was dreadful. I needed to see him, be with him, hug him.

Oscar's condition encroached on my life with such force that I wondered how I was going to stay strong for him and the rest of my worried family. The pressure Archie was under was horrendous, as he worked hard to get the score needed for the university course he wanted to do. I was helpless to alleviate his worry, knowing the best I could do was be there for him whenever he needed me.

Archie's Year Twelve formal came around, and he looked so handsome in his suit. Unfortunately, Oscar was unable to attend and it broke Archie's heart. The rest of us attended to celebrate this big milestone with him. Lots of photos were taken to text to Oscar, always including him as best we could.

I went to see Oscar. He was in good spirits, the medication to relieve his pain was working, and he was able to go for a walk outside his ward. Oscar had his laptop with him. He asked me, "Grandma, would you be able to help me with my TAFE homework?"

"Sure can, sweetheart, although I don't know how much help I will be."

"That's okay. If you can read the questions to me, that would be a big help."

"I can do that, honey."

Oscar finally had the biopsy. A week later, he was diagnosed with an astrocytoma brain tumour, which starts in cells called astrocytes. They support and connect nerve cells in the brain and spinal cord. The tumour wasn't round like a ball. It had tentacles, which attached to both frontal lobes of his brain.

The whole family were absolutely devastated. Oscar was allowed to come back to the Sunshine Coast after he received his diagnosis, but he wasn't allowed to drive for six months. Any sort of brain surgery can cause tiredness as well as feeling confused, disorientated and clumsy (called post-operative dizziness). Coordination, balance and thinking skills can also be affected.

That was very upsetting for him as he loved driving and being independent. Oscar and Archie always went to car shows, the movies, and just drove around as young men do. The silver lining was that Archie had his licence, so he took the lead and was able to drive them to places of interest, keeping some form of normality in both their lives.

A couple of days after Oscar came home, the grandboys came for a visit. The usual shenanigans ensued – lunch, a movie and great company filled our afternoon. It was wonderful for us all to keep doing something that felt normal. Choosing what to watch on TV, we chose car shows, which I enjoyed also, leaving my Chrises for another time. Having my amazing, loving grandboys here helped me stay grounded. Hannah was in constant contact with photos or videos of our little Ivy.

Having video chats with this precious little being was so therapeutic for me.

By 2023, my list of parts had grown exponentially. During my psychology sessions, up to four parts could present together. Each with their own traumatic memory to deal with. Emotions ran rampant during these sessions, leaving me exhausted, bewildered and sometimes still in denial. Declaring I was not coming back for any more sessions. *Ever.*

Having many different parts is termed as co-consciousness. It means I have two or more parts present in my body at once or become aware of the outside world simultaneously. My psychologist has told me I don't just have four or even ten or twenty parts. I have many, many parts (sometimes described as 'polyfragmented') and she believes she hasn't met them all yet.

Using EMDR, my parts – who think they are still in the trauma when it happened years ago – are helped to understand they are now much older and they are safe. They share my consciousness in real time. Tommy, for example, is now co-conscious. As a result, I have not had the need to punch someone's lights out. Instead, I use my words.

Remember that car crash on my 12th birthday? It left me consumed by guilt. *If only I had chosen differently on that fateful day.* I knew logically I didn't cause the car crash. But the ugly truth is that I was already scarred by worthlessness, and, over the years, I had found it extremely hard to forgive myself.

As I have already explained, it is hardwired into my brain that I am to blame for everything – a leftover reaction to my father's verbal abuse. So, to let this one go – and not blame myself for the devastating car crash – is overwhelmingly difficult for me.

Amelia, a 12-year-old part, is holding this memory. During a psychology session, she was extremely upset, blaming herself repeatedly for the car crash. Amelia kept saying if she had made a different decision and if it wasn't her birthday, the crash wouldn't have happened. Her sisters and her grandma wouldn't have been hurt. She was convinced that it was her fault because the lady wouldn't have slapped her across the face if it wasn't. Amelia's uncontrollable sobbing was heartbreaking to experience. My psychologist had to speak gently, reassuring her that it wasn't her fault and explaining the reasons why.

Amelia knew that at one point directly after the crash, still trapped in the car, I had stood on Susie trying to get out – a detail that only came out during this session. The guilt she was holding on to was all-encompassing. She was so distraught that all my psychologist could do was get her to do the butterfly hug.

Did me standing on Susie cause her internal injuries?

Over the years, I had remembered everything else about the crash, but I had no recollection of standing on Susie. Amelia had kept this detail from me because it would have been too painful to hold. If I had known this at the time of the crash, I know I would not have coped. I was already struggling. I feel this information may have sent me over the edge. Maybe even pushing me to have my first suicidal thoughts as a 12-year-old.

My psychologist helped me to realise my extreme reaction to car fumes would have come from the car crash. Screeching brakes, metal on metal, spilt fuel, exhaust fumes. Following this session, I was overwhelmed with emotional exhaustion. I went home and went straight to bed, hoping sleep would come easily.

Amelia presented at my next session to share another memory – of my father abusing my mother. While Amelia was sobbing uncontrollably, her heart was palpitating. Once again, my psychologist was able to calm Amelia down with the butterfly hug, reassuring her that we were no longer in that moment. Her feeling of guilt was overwhelming. My psychologist reassured her that she was only young and would not have been able to help her mum, which helped her to reconnect to the present moment.

As I said before, everything my parts feel and experience, I do too. After a very traumatic session, where one or more memories are presented, I am absolutely spent. Crying for almost 45 minutes at a time is extremely tiring, too. Amelia is also terrified of loud noises. I wonder if Amelia being terrified of loud noises doesn't only come from hearing mum and dad fighting. Could it also be a reaction to hearing ambulance and fire truck sirens on the day of the car crash?

One day, while I was sitting in my lounge room, it felt like the traffic outside was becoming louder and louder. My hypersensitivity skyrocketed. An adult inner voice I didn't recognise was provoking me. This extremely scary part was egging me on to hurt myself. I could feel the absolute disdain this part had for me. I called him "The Intimidator". *Do it, do it, hurt yourself. It will make you feel better. Don't be such a wimp. Cut yourself – you want to see the blood. Do it.* I had an army of people in my head yelling at me. Some were angry, some were trying to protect me, and others were frightened by what was going on.

My hands started to flail around, twitching uncontrollably as I struggled to pick up the nail file. Stabbing my arm numerous times, I felt no pain. I watched on as "The Intimidator" made holes in my flesh. *Doesn't that feel better? I am helping you. See what I have done? You aren't a wimp after all.* Blood started to trickle down my arm. All I could do was stare, emotionless, at my bleeding arm. *What is going on? I have never had a part talk to me like this before.*

All of a sudden, a rush of absolute heart-pumping fear took over. I was crying hysterically. Still present to witness all that was happening to me, Amelia, who holds so many horrific traumas, sat in my chair, shaking like a leaf in a wild storm. Memories flooded my mind. I couldn't stop them. I couldn't control what was happening. Amelia was so firmly planted in my world that I struggled to bring myself forward. I was fearful because I had once again lost control. *How am I going to get out of this? I am trapped. I am so scared. I am on my own. I need to get her attention. How? How?*

I tried to remember all the things my psychologist taught me to help me come out of a dissociative episode. *I need to talk to her and make her realise she isn't in the trauma anymore.* I started talking softly to Amelia.

"It is okay. You are safe. I am here to protect you. You are safe. Look at our hands."

I put my old hands up in front of me as I continued to talk to this terrified part of me.

"See? You aren't young anymore. You have grown up. They are an old person's hands, wrinkled. No one can hurt you anymore. You are grown up. You are an adult now."

I looked around my lounge room, stopping at photos of my family.

"Look at these photos. They are your family. You have two children, three grandchildren and one great-granddaughter. You are a lot older now and you can look after yourself. You are safe. I will not let anything happen to you."

I could feel Amelia starting to calm down. *Thank god it is working.* It took more than 15 minutes for this part of me to de-escalate. At a previous session with my psychologist, we had made a room in my mind where my parts can go to feel safe. We called it "The Safe Room". It is a huge, welcoming room with large windows, allowing lots of light and sunshine in. Comfy bean bags and lounge chairs are scattered around the room. There are children's tables and chairs, with toys and games. Bookshelves are ladened with many different books, both children's and adults'. All of this is to help my parts to feel safe and ultimately in control.

"You can go to 'The Safe Room' and relax if you like. Thank you for helping me all these years. I love you."

My psychologist has always said we do EMDR therapy to help my parts to integrate – never to get rid of them. When my parts are integrated with me, my past traumas are not triggered by situations in my present life.

On more than one occasion, a part would ask, "Why do you want to get rid of me?"

The answer that my psychologist always gives is, "I do not want to get rid of you. Jo needs you, so you will always be with her. You are a valuable part of Jo and have done a marvellous job to keep her safe. Now that she has grown into a woman who can look after herself, it is your turn to relax and do what you would like to do."

Sometimes it takes a few sessions for my parts to understand what is being said to them. As my parts come forward and talk to my psychologist, realising they don't have to protect me anymore, they are relieved. Some cry because they are so exhausted from always being switched on, ready to help me at a moment's notice. The younger ones want to go and play in "The Safe Room". Knowing they have done a wonderful job over the years, now they are allowed to go and enjoy themselves and be happy.

I proceeded to dress my wounds as I reflected on what just happened. This dissociative episode was the worst I had ever experienced on my own so far. It came on so quickly and violently, I was left exhausted. Not knowing the trigger that escalated the traffic noise was annoying. My triggers can be so subtle or they can hit me like a sledgehammer. I was also relieved that I was able to help myself overcome a particularly scary and debilitating situation. It showed that I was, hopefully, finally, becoming the master of my parts. Although "The Intimidator" is a worry.

I was having regular appointments trying to keep the momentum going, helping my parts to realise they were not in trauma anymore. During the session, I mentioned the dissociative episode I'd had at home. This triggered another part to present to talk about the memory they held. It was a nightmare for me.

All I wanted to do was escape, shrink, go to sleep and never wake up again.

Little Chloe, who is only five years old, was so upset about how my niece, Katherine, was treated at the family barbeque. She was in the background while Miss Angry, Mum and Dad were arguing. Chloe was scared, crying uncontrollably, and also angry because people were not loving each other. Chloe had experienced many years of arguments, wishing only for harmony and peace to fill her world.

My mind was always on Oscar. He was improving and cleared to go back to work. His bosses and workmates were delighted to have him back. However, he was told unequivocally that if he needed to rest or go home, he should do so. It was heartwarming to see a bunch of men so invested in making Oscar's working life as easy as possible. It was great therapy for Oscar to keep working for as long as he could.

Kylie took Oscar to the Sunshine Coast University Hospital (SCUH) for his initial tests with the radiology department. The results were sent away to Sydney for more analysis. Mid-October, the results came back. Oscar was further diagnosed with diffuse paediatric high-grade glioma, which is a collection of brain tumours in children or young adults. Traditionally, there was an extremely poor clinical outcome. Archie visited after we were told all this. We were both devastated and wondered how Oscar would be feeling, knowing he may not achieve all the things he wanted to do in his lifetime.

A treatment plan was devised for Oscar: 33 radiation treatments, some chemo treatments and regular blood tests. But only on business days – weekends were for resting. Oscar was able to have all his treatments at SCUH, which was a godsend for him and all the family.

At Oscar's first radiation appointment, he was given his treatment identification number along with information about available appointment times. The receptionist explained how everything would work and how to fill out the appointment schedule. Armed with this information, we grabbed a seat together and proceeded to fill out the paperwork.

“I want to keep working, Grandma.”

“Great, sweetheart. Are you wanting morning or afternoon appointments?’

“It doesn’t matter. Can we make some early in the morning so I can go to work afterwards?”

“Okay. Yes, there are some times available on different days in the morning. Do these look good?’

“That’s good, Grandma.”

“There are some during the afternoon and some still available after work. I will take those too.”

“Great, Grandma. I will take a photo of our form so I can show work.”

“Good idea, sweetheart. I will too so I can put all the times in my diary. We are all sorted.”

Clinton, the service manager for Sunshine Toyota at Sippy Downs, was more than happy for Oscar to be at work whenever he could. Oscar’s bosses and workmates were always a tower of strength and compassion for Oscar’s changing needs.

The radiation treatments only took around 15 minutes, but, like all hospital appointments, the waiting times were sometimes long. It was a “hurry up and wait” scenario. Oscar and I used that time to chat about whatever came to mind or look at crazy stuff on our phones. I was just happy to feel him sitting next to me.

When Oscar had important doctor appointments, Kylie would take him. His dad, Brett, would come up from Brisbane as well to speak with the doctor. Oscar was soldiering on. He was having oncology reviews and radiation reviews to track the progress of the treatments.

Hannah and Ivy had come up to visit. Ivy was six months old and a delight to be around – a welcomed, happy distraction. Oscar, Hannah, Ivy and Archie came to my place for lunch one day. It was magical to have all my grandchildren and great-granddaughter together with me. Hannah made a “Welcome, Daddy” sign for Ivy to hold when they went to Brisbane Airport to pick up Marc. Lots of laughs and cuddles were shared during that precious visit.

By mid-November, it was time for Archie’s graduation ceremony. Oscar had a radiation treatment, but we made it on time for the 6pm start. Being able to see Archie receive his graduation certificate was great.

I was on a downward spiral. I was worried about Oscar’s parents. *This is the second time they have had to watch their son fight cancer. I wish I could help them. Take their relentless fear and pain away.*

The whole family was suffering from the impact of Oscar’s devastating diagnoses.

CHAPTER 19

Identity

I am many parts and connected to none
Constantly alert, just wanting to run
Days, hours, minutes remembered or forgotten
Good or bad, feeling downtrodden
Trigger becomes the go-to word
Unable to settle, a flighty bird
Despair shadows my every thought
Depression I have always fought
DID diagnosed, my new norm
Am I saved or sitting in the eye of the storm?
Once through the eye, healing or friction
Bringing to tears my new conviction

—Jo Wilcox

Holidays are not my best friend, especially the Christmas school holidays. As a child, a lot of the abuse and domestic issues escalated at this time. More parties, more celebrations, more visitors, more alcohol consumption all blended to make the perfect storm. A mixture of happiness and abuse, laughter and tears, I never knew what was going to happen next. Sleep evaded me, peace bypassed me, leaving me in a state of stress.

The car crash that happened on my 12th birthday also occurred during these holidays. Summer in Australia is hot and muggy. The heat alone triggers memories and has done every summer of my life. Living in the country, summertime was unrelenting. Temperatures could get as high as 45 degrees Celsius, over 110 degrees Fahrenheit. No air conditioning, no fly screens – we just put up with it. From a very young age, I have associated hot weather with pain and trauma. As an adult, keeping as busy as I can helps me to navigate my turbulent emotional state. Watching my loving grandson, Oscar, battle cancer for the second time made dealing with my summer triggers harder than ever before.

One summer's day, as I was mowing the lawn, I started to sob, mumbling continuously, "I don't want to do this." I couldn't see where I was mowing as tears and sweat blurred my vision. I thought to myself: *it is just the heat. I am exhausted. I'll be right.* While trying to wipe my eyes clear, my mind meandered back decades. "I don't want to do this." I was so upset I almost passed out. I laid down on the lawn in the foetal position, repeating over and over again, "I don't want to do this." I was having a dissociative episode. A part was out and too terrified to speak. Thoughts raced around in my head. *Am I having a stroke? I have overdone it. Too much stress and sadness for too long.*

Lying motionless on the grass, I tried to slow my breathing. *I have to calm this part down.* All I could find the strength to do was talk. “You are safe. You are safe. You aren’t in danger. You have grown up. You are an adult now.” I kept talking, reassuring her no one would ever hurt her again. Thankfully, I felt the part calming down. I could move my arms and legs – I wasn’t in a brain fog anymore. I laid on the grass for a few more minutes. Then I sat up, leaning against a tree. I was absolutely exhausted.

I was astonished how debilitating this episode was, not only mentally but physically as well. I hope one day this part will present when I am in a session so she can be helped.

Sleep deprivation and my constant triggers wear me down. At times, nothing can console me – not even the thoughts of my children, grandchildren or my dear friends. My depression takes hold of me, reluctant to release its vice-like grip. Negative emotions cloud my future and diminish my ability to see anything but failure and disappointment as my legacy.

My many parts argue about what chaotic safeguard they will employ to keep me safe. One will want me to self-harm. One will want me to go to bed and hide under my covers while keeping really quiet. One will have me scream at the top of my lungs and maybe, just maybe, one will kill me off.

A positive thought pattern begets a positive life. I do believe if we can project happiness, and wear a smile regularly, that would quickly become our go-to emotion. A habit, pattern or belief born from the threat of pain, humiliation or perceived death quickly becomes a suit of armour worn bravely, with only one goal: to keep you safe. It is not easy to become armour free if your go-to emotion for years has been fear.

Easy becomes: cleaning and polishing the twisted, battered, war-torn armour that is your protection. Your second skin and your first line of defence.

Hard becomes: breaking the habit or pattern, which is close to impossible, leading you to believe that every inanimate object or living thing is a threat and you will die. Or, worse, that he will find you, if you let your guard down and crack that beautiful smile, or, heaven forbid, allow yourself to feel happiness in all its glory.

Fear can override any positive emotion. If fear captures your smile and lassoes your happiness, your ability to see your life – past, present or future – in a positive light is screwed. All the negativity that sits stagnant throughout your body becomes its own weapon. Pushing the wielder to viciously turn it on themselves. Wanting to be rid of this paralysing energy becomes so strong that a plan is hatched to harm the body that houses the pain. Smash the windows and kick in the doors, hoping to find some relief.

We all have days, even weeks, where nothing goes right. Where one thing after another builds the pressure to explosive proportions. My pressure gauge is always in the danger zone, leaving my tipping point easy to reach. Money issues, relationships issues, housing issues are constant flag raisers for me. My kryptonite is my self-hatred. This beast is formidable. Making sure I always feel inadequate, unlovable, full of shame and guilt, ugly and worthless. That I am broken beyond repair and should be unceremoniously thrown on the rubbish heap.

One minute, I am moving through my day. Next, I am strapped into the seat of my emotional roller coaster, screaming and hanging on for grim death as I hurtle towards the bottom of my black hole. It is within these moments that my fear becomes my conductor. She decides how long my ride will be hours – days or weeks. How many twists and turns I will encounter and whether the churning in my stomach will leave me literally throwing up or only mentally overwhelmed, unable to see a way out of another fractured mess.

Physically, my body can also react. Pain, diarrhoea, shaking and tiredness are just a few of the symptoms. Wanting to bury my emotions can also cause me to binge eat, causing sugar-induced headaches or vomiting. Daily routines feel like I am walking through molasses.

Emotional instability becomes my life, while illogical thinking rules my mind.

Oscar's horrendous journey plays out constantly in my mind. I am useless to help him, way out of my depth.

Why am I still alive and Oscar so sick? It should be me, not him. It is not fair.

Over the years since starting therapy, I have attended many workshops run by a sexual assault service. I have met many amazing women who have survived their own journeys of sexual assault, domestic violence and many other abuses.

I enjoy monthly art therapy classes the most. My childhood and teenage years were filled with art. However, art of any kind has strong associations for me. Art was my go-to when my home life was unpredictable and scary. Drawing and painting were my escape. My eyes saw only beautiful colours, my mind thought only in terms of brush, paint and pencil selections, and my heart felt peace only while I was locked away in my little bedroom.

To start creating art again wasn't an easy ask. Memories of raised voices and angry words were all I could think of while I sat in a welcoming room with ladies who only wanted the best for me. I struggled to hold back tears sometimes, to not show my inner turmoil while I painted, drew, cut out, glued and put together my own masterpieces.

Many funny and awkward conversations were had while we took time for ourselves. We saw ourselves in a different light, happy and content to sit in our own wisdom and create. A couple of hours of oneness before we all had to venture back into our daily lives.

Archie had received his ATAR score, which was high enough to do the degrees he wanted to at QUT. With Oscar's health causing Archie so much worry, it was wonderful to know that he could put the school year behind him and concentrate on being with his big brother as much as possible.

Unfortunately, Oscar became unwell and had to be admitted to hospital. I was helping him get ready. Brett and Archie were also on their way. Oscar's cancer care nurse rang and told Oscar and me that she was going to get an ambulance to pick him up.

"Grandma, I don't want to go in the ambulance. You will be able to take me, won't you?"

"Yes, sweetheart, of course. I can definitely take you."

I relayed that message to the nurse, so she gave instructions on where I was to take Oscar when we arrived. She would be waiting with a wheelchair for him.

After hanging up, I said to Oscar, "The internal stairs are going to be a problem, sweetheart, but we will manage. I will go first, and you can go down on your bottom, one step at a time, behind me. How will that be?"

"No probs, Grandma. We will manage together."

"Okay, sweetheart."

I was getting Oscar's gear together when Archie and Brett arrived. I was so relieved as they were able to help Oscar down the stairs and into Brett's car. I relayed the nurse's message to Brett, so he knew where to go when they got to the hospital. I gave Oscar a big hug and a kiss before watching Brett drive Oscar to hospital.

Christmas was only a few days away, so Archie and I went shopping, braving the jostling crowds as we chose presents for our family. A few days before Christmas Oscar was having an MRI to check on his progress after finishing all his radiation treatments. Kylie and Brett both attended this meeting. More devastating news – the radiation treatments hadn't worked. The original tumour had grown and a new, smaller tumour had developed.

Receiving this diagnoses shattered any hope I had that Oscar could beat this life-threatening disease. As it grew larger, the tumour was slowly robbing Oscar of his sight and speech. By the end of December

2023 my family and I knew the incomprehensible truth that our precious Oscar had only three months to live.

How does a 21-year-old young man deal with such devastating news?

My heart was breaking for Oscar. Trying to stay as calm as possible while in Oscar's company was nerve wracking. Wanting to hug him and never let go made my heart ache. Wanting to take his pain away riddled me with guilt for something I had no control over. I wanted to take his place so he could experience a long and healthy life.

How was I going to prepare to lose my grandson?

The next day, I picked up Archie and we went to visit Oscar at SCUH. Guy and Sarah came also. It was wonderful to see them. Oscar was very weak, but responsive. He was eating well but the dizziness and blurred vision were still a problem for him.

Oscar was allowed to come home for Christmas Day. It was heartwarming to have him home with all the family. It was a beautiful day. Brett, Iris and her two kids Connor and Katie came up to Kylie's as well. Many photos were taken of us all together. Oscar received many hugs and kisses before he had to go back to hospital in the evening.

On Boxing Day, I visited Oscar in hospital on my own.

"Hello, sweetheart. How are you feeling today?"

"Not too bad, Grandma. My eyes are getting worse though."

"Sweetheart, you know if I could take your place, I would. I don't know how I am going to cope without you."

I started to cry as Oscar and I held hands.

"I know, Grandma. I love you so much. You have always been there for me."

"You have to let me know that you are okay. That you are happy and well. Can you do that for me? Send me a message if you can, letting me know that you are okay, sweetheart."

"I will, Grandma. I will."

We talked some more about all sorts of things. Over the years, Oscar and I have talked about spirituality. "Woo-woo", as he would call it.

From the first day Oscar was in hospital until the day he lost his sight and ability to speak, I texted him jokes. I wanted him to have a happy moment in his otherwise challenging day. I needed to stay connected to him as I could not always go and see him for various reasons. It was our time together.

I spent hours trying to find jokes that would make Oscar laugh. Of course, he was a young man, and I was an old lady. Oscar would text back after receiving each joke.

> **Jeez, Grandma, you can do better than that. The challenge is on. Get your funny cap on, Grandma.**

> **Okay, Oscar, watch this space. You will be laughing so hard you will pee your pants.**

Sometimes, what he thought was funny and what I thought was funny were very different. Many times, though, I hit the mark.

Good one, Grandma, good one. That is funny.

It occurred to me that Oscar needed to have a will, an enduring power of attorney (EPA) and an advance health directive (AHD) drawn up. *How do I broach this subject with him? How do I talk about my precious Oscar dying? How can I talk about paperwork at a time like this?* I was so conflicted. I didn't want to upset Oscar, but he needed to get his affairs in order.

I taught Oscar, Hannah and Archie how to open bank accounts, get their tax file numbers, obtain Medicare cards, and organise anything else they needed to start adulting. I knew in my heart Oscar would understand that this needed to happen. One day, I bit the bullet and had the heartbreaking conversation with Oscar.

"Sweetheart, I need to talk to you about getting certain bits of paperwork done." I explained the different documents to him.

"Grandma, why do I have to do this? I don't have anything."

"You do have things, sweetheart. You have your car, money in the bank and you have your superannuation as well as your personal effects. These all have to be looked after."

"Okay, Grandma. I will think about it."

I could see by the look on Oscar's face that this was a huge task for someone so young to take on board.

"Oscar, I will help you do all of these things. You know I will always be here for you. We will sort all of this out together. Okay, sweetheart? I am happy to be the executor of your estate, Oscar. I will be with you every inch of the way. I love you very much – you know that."

"Yes, I know you do, Grandma. I love you heaps too. Yes, I want you to look after everything for me."

"Okay, sweetheart. I will do that."

I left the conversation there. It would take Oscar a bit of time to digest what I had just spoken to him about. With all the other horrendous things he had to deal with, it was unfair he had to deal with this as well. Later that afternoon, Oscar came home to Kylie's and was classed as an outpatient.

On New Year's Eve, we all gathered at Kylie's for morning tea. I was playing on the floor with Ivy. As I was getting up, Oscar came over to me, looked lovingly into my eyes, took my hand and helped me up.

We held hands for what seemed like an eternity before we let go and had the longest hug together. No words were spoken.

I started to prepare Oscar's end-of-life documentation. I learnt Oscar could prepare his own will. I decided to forgo the EPA and AHD. In Oscar's case, there was no way I was going to put him through such an emotional and tiring time, gathering medical documentation and visiting doctors. I would help Oscar write a letter in which he would state his wishes for the end of his life.

Archie brought Oscar up to my place to work on his documents. I sat facing them, ready to document the day's chat. This was the hardest thing I have ever done – sitting across from my 21-year-old grandson, whom I adored, asking him questions about the end of his life.

Archie was such a treasure that day. His compassion and computer skills helped us gather Oscar's passwords for his various accounts. Hard questions had to be asked. To be the executor of Oscar's estate, I had to know and be able to access his entire life. My grandsons were the bravest young men in the world on that extremely emotional day. With Oscar's will and letter of wishes finished and ready to be typed up, Archie took Oscar home as he was exhausted.

Once Oscar's documents were all signed and witnessed, I sent them off to all the appropriate places. Organising his cremation was extremely emotional for me. Never in a million years would I have dreamt that I would be organising such things for my grandson. Life is cruel.

Oscar was classed as palliative. Kylie had stopped working so she could care for Oscar at home. Her heartache, knowing that Oscar was going to leave her, would have been excruciating. Each day, with the help of her caring husband, Kylie was there, loving Oscar until he needed more intensive care and was admitted to a palliative care facility.

Sitting on the side of the bed, cupping Oscar's face in my hands and wiping away both our tears, was surreal. My heart connected energetically with his, aching, missing beats and struggling to comprehend what was inevitable. A hug that didn't last long enough ripped my soul apart. My loving grandson, my friend, my partner in crime was leaving me forever. In a whispered voice, I said my last goodbye. "I love you, I love you, I love you, Oscar."

I didn't want to let go, but I knew I had to. I had to get up and walk away. I had to allow other family members their time to say goodbye. I was broken. As I left Oscar's room, sobbing uncontrollably, my only thought was: *how is Oscar feeling? Is he struggling? Is he in pain? Is he hurting? Is he frightened?* The bravest young man, whom I will love forever, would soon be sleeping peacefully.

Oscar passed away at the beginning of March 2024 with all his family around him.

No more photos to take, no more history to make. Just sadness and disbelief.

It only took six short months for this insidious disease to rob my amazing, caring grandson of his future. He never gave up, fighting valiantly. Oscar's caring, respectful and friendly nature touched a lot of people. This was seen at his memorial. Family, friends of family, school friends, teachers, work bosses and workmates all came together to celebrate the life of a compassionate, kind and thoughtful young man.

I am so blessed to have had Oscar choose me to be his grandma. *Oscar, you will always be in my heart. Love you always and forever. See you in my dreams, sweetheart.*

CHAPTER 20

Grief

My heart skips a beat, leaving me unable to catch my breath,
while my blouse catches tears of sadness as they roll off my chin.
What is this unfamiliar feeling holding me captive?
My mind is struggling to comprehend what my eyes are seeing.
I have forgotten how to sleep, only tossing and turning,
wishing I knew if you were happy and healthy in heaven.
My waking moments are filled with unanswered questions,
as memories of your smile, your voice and
your loving hugs make me smile.
Another tear gently leaves a trail of sadness over my cheek.
Grief has made its home in every cell of my body,
robbing me of my will to live without you.
Will the pain I feel ever leave? Will my heart ever mend?
Will my eyes be smiling eyes once again?

—Jo Wilcox

Grief is debilitating. I hadn't been sleeping, even though I just wanted to go to bed and forget I lived in this world. I was constantly thinking about things I could have done for Oscar. I was stuck on Oscar's memorial. I didn't have a formal speech written. I didn't think I would be able to get up on my own and speak in front of a crowd of people. On the day, many beautifully worded speeches were given about Oscar's life. The crowd was asked if anyone else would like to speak. I wanted to, but I was so emotional I didn't think I could. My friend, Lyn, gave me a nudge.

"Go on, Jo, you can do this. Go on."

I got up and started to tell stories about my life with my grandchildren. My emotions were running wild throughout my body, and my mind was cluttered with so many words I wanted to say. I started to feel overwhelmed. After expressing how much I would always love Oscar, I handed the microphone back.

The familiar self-destructive talk started. *Why didn't you keep talking? Why didn't you tell everyone about happy times you shared with Oscar? You are a waste of space*. I didn't say how I took Oscar to weekly rugby training sessions in Brisbane. I didn't say how Oscar and I kicked the footy and paddled at the beach when he was recovering from leukaemia. I didn't say how I taught him to drive. I didn't say how many special memories I had of the two of us together. I wanted everyone to know how precious Oscar was to me, but I didn't. I *couldn't*.

I missed speaking with many people who attended Oscar's memorial. Not because I didn't want to. My thinking process was so out of whack, I felt so disconnected from reality. It never entered my head to mingle, converse and show my gratitude to everyone for coming. I was lost, trapped on my own island of confusion. I want to give my deepest apology to those wonderful people, including family and friends who

I didn't speak with. I was not ignoring you, I saw you, and I thank you from the bottom of my heart for your love and support on a day when we were all hurting.

I stumbled through life like a robot. The numbness I felt hurt. Why? Numbness by definition doesn't have a feeling. It is a void. My eyes saw only sadness. My heart sat in my chest like stone. My logical mind was shattered. I was done. Done fighting, done apologising, done smiling when I wanted to cry, done moving when I wanted to stay in the same position, done being controlled. I did not know what more I could do to help myself ride out my debilitating mental health issues.

The layers of pain and grief weaving their way through my everyday life left me incapable of moving forward. When happiness becomes my enemy, it ignites a fear so profound that embracing sadness as my friend is all that is left. Passions, dreams and aspirations flicker aimlessly in the distance. I have walked many kilometres through thick undergrowth and, occasionally, clear, beautiful fields, but never see that flicker grow any larger. I know I am strong, resilient and tenacious. I am able to rise above disasters and horrendous pain to face another day. I also know I can be my own worst enemy, putting myself in harm's way, wanting to end it all, leaving behind all the unfinished masterpieces of melancholy and despair.

My life has been mine and mine alone to navigate. Although I know I am loved by my family, my CPTSD sucks the life out of me, leaving a shell of vulnerability. The ripple effect of hopelessness, worthlessness, self-doubt overshadows everything I do, everything I think and everything I say. Add in depressive toxicity, which oozes through every vein of my body, and I am left knowing that I am nothing but shit on the shoe of society.

My psychology sessions became even harder to deal with. If my psychologist was working with a part and asked them if they knew about Oscar passing, their answer was yes, and they would start crying. I was in a constant state of emotional madness. I told my psychologist about my self-hatred over what I didn't say at Oscar's memorial. She explained to me that it was a coping mechanism so I wouldn't go to a place of absolute grief and despair.

I didn't want to feel the pain – not just from Oscar passing, but also from my past traumas. I understood what she was saying to me. If I allowed myself to feel the pain, I would be vulnerable. If I was vulnerable, I would be taken advantage of, which would lead to more pain. I do not remember grieving for the past that I experienced, for the abuses I suffered, for the lost childhood I will never get back, for the people I loved and lost, or for any other losses I endured.

My psychologist got me to do the butterfly hug. She got me to think about Oscar and the love I had for him – how I missed him terribly and wanted him back. I started to cry a little. The more I tapped my arms, the more I cried. Then the floodgates opened and memories of loss exploded in my mind.

I was completely open and vulnerable as I cried tears that were over 60 years old. Tears that had been held back by a wall of sheer determination and tenacity.

This session changed me, allowing me to grieve without fear of being hurt. I experienced a small shift that day. Whatever emotions that stopped me from expressing my sadness in the past became pliable, making it easier for me to express my feelings.

I have always believed in the afterlife – that we choose to reincarnate, time and time again. Although, for me, I wonder why on earth I decided to put myself through such stress, sadness and debilitating mental health problems this time around.

Oscar kept his word and has visited me on numerous occasions. Being Oscar's executor, I had his mobile phone and laptop in my possession. I had cancelled his mobile plan, leaving his phone unable to send or receive texts or phone calls. One day, I was watching TV when I received a text from Oscar's mobile number. I stared at my phone, thinking: *this cannot be happening. Oscar's mobile doesn't work anymore. I have his mobile, it is in the cupboard, no one could be using it.* I ran to make sure it was in the cupboard. Yes, it was. *It doesn't work. Shit.* I looked at this message again, making sure I hadn't dreamt it. I took a screenshot because no one would believe me if I told them. My mind was going into overwhelm, trying to make sense of what I had just received.

Oscar loved cars. The faster and noisier, the better. A friend of Brett's had sports cars. Oscar, Archie and Brett would visit him. The grandboys were able to sit in the wonderful cars he had in his garage. The text I received had two photos, which were the same, of Oscar sitting in the passenger seat of this amazing car, with the door open. The smile he had on his face was ecstatic.

When Oscar passed away, no one could tell me the exact time he passed – only that it was sometime between midday and 1pm. I received this text at 12:27pm. I had goose bumps all over my body. I started crying tears of joy, knowing that this was Oscar letting me know he was okay, very happy and healthy. "Major woo-woo," as Oscar would say.

I have had other funny things happen, like lights being turned on and off. In the middle of the night when I couldn't sleep, I would see a bright light in my bedroom. I have also felt Oscar kiss me on my cheek while I lay in bed. During all of these experiences, I would be enveloped in healing and the feeling of tremendous love.

Healing comes in many forms. One thing I have learnt throughout my lifetime is to allow myself to experience different modalities that I felt resonated with my inner child and soul. We are all different. Some find their solace in going to church, some find it in spiritual healing circles, some find it through their own expression of creativity. My philosophy is to allow everyone to do what makes them happy. There is no right or wrong. There is, hopefully, only peace for our souls through our choices, and connection with likeminded people.

I was lucky to have my dear friend, Lyn, invite me to a spiritual retreat in Maleny in the Sunshine Coast hinterland. It had only been five months since Oscar passed, so I wasn't sure if I could be somewhere new and surrounded by people I did not know. I was so pleased I did push through my fears as I arrived at this welcoming place of spiritual refreshment. It was called White Eagle Lodge.

Gay and Lyn (a different Lyn), who were running the retreat, were so welcoming. I was put at ease and fortunate to be participating, as they had a special guest. Jenny, a global leader of the lodge, was visiting Australia and facilitating alongside Gay and Lyn. Jenny spoke about what other lodges throughout the world are doing to help individuals as well as humanitarian organisations survive in the sometimes turbulent times of our planet and its inhabitants.

Over six days, I learnt that White Eagle teaching is based on a simple yet profound, heart-centred philosophy, which brings with it the light and radiance of the spiritual world. It provides very practical support in day-to-day living. It also helps many people find answers to some of the most difficult questions of human existence. What is the purpose of life? What happens after death? Are healing miracles possible? Is there something I can do to help heal the world? Through wise and gentle teachings, its aim is to facilitate loving understanding among all people and for all living things, bringing a sense of inner peace and wellbeing.

Throughout the retreat, I participated in peaceful and enlightened meditations where I felt Oscar's presence. With my eyes closed and my heart open, I could see him standing, healed and happy, behind me. The love I felt in my heart radiated throughout my body as Oscar put his hands on my shoulders. I was gently crying tears of joy as I experienced his unconditional love and saw his happy smile once again.

In between meditations and other enjoyable activities, I ate way too much yummy food and met friendly people from all walks of life. All while enjoying colourful sunsets in the most tranquil surroundings. If I hadn't overcome my fears, I would have missed out on new friendships, healing and connecting with Oscar's love. I left the retreat feeling at peace with my world, and with a better understanding of the grieving and healing process in front of me.

I know that my mental health issues will be with me until I cross over and see Oscar again. We will again be constant companions, sitting on a cloud, telling each other crazy jokes while eating snacks.

Allowing myself the freedom to experience new things isn't always possible. Worrying about what may happen because of my DID can be debilitating. I have to give my parts some leeway though, as they are the ones who shield me from the atrocities inflicted upon my body and soul. Fighting for my safety at every turn.

Never dropping the baton,
never quitting the race.

The more I worked with my psychologist, the more different parts presented. Frightened, angry, overwhelmed and courageous parts opened up, in some cases for the first time, relaying details of events. Unbelievable secrets had been kept from me for many years. Events that I had no prior knowledge of shattered my world as each part courageously bared their soul, releasing the emotional trauma they endured.

When they present, some parts may tell their story, whereas others are so distraught they say nothing at all and leave. It is wonderful if a part can be integrated more and more into the now by using EMDR.

My parts look after each other, too. There is Harper, who is five years old, and June, who is 13 years old, who look after Miss Hide. Many other pairings of my parts have become evident as well. It is an incredible network of helpers, protectors and holders of traumatic memories.

Many other parts have presented since the initial ones made themselves known to my bewildered but brave massage therapist back in 2000. You have met a few of them throughout my book. I have made notes from most of my psychology sessions. When I looked back through six years of diary and journal entries, I remembered most of my sessions. But some I didn't remember and I was surprised all over again by what I read.

During a session, an older lady, named Violet, and Mia, who was a baby, presented. Violet cared for Mia, who was too young to talk but was emotionally distraught, crying uncontrollably. My psychologist tapped on my knees, as the baby cried and cried. Violet told us Mia wouldn't let her tell us about the memory they both held, as it was too traumatic. As Mia calmed down, I took over from my psychologist, resting my hands on my knees, and started to alternatively tap the top of them. The rhythm and sensation helped Mia to self-soothe. While doing this, my psychologist talked gently and calmly to Mia, letting her know she was safe and not in trauma anymore.

Knee tapping is another variation of EMDR. It has the same effect as a butterfly hug. Because Mia the baby was so distraught, butterfly hugging wasn't an option. Knee tapping creates an alternating left-to-right stimulation that engages both sides of the brain, helping to soothe Mia as well as doing some memory reprocessing,

There are parts who are in a role of authority. "The Manager" part, who is very strong emotionally and a good source of information, has presented more than once to oversee the sessions. He has told my psychologist that there is a whole new cluster of parts around the betrayal and mistrust I endured before, during and after the demise of both the businesses and homes and the immense loss I had to deal with. *That will be fun when we get around to hearing from them, I am sure.*

An older part, who calls herself "The Librarian" presented. She is very strict and strong-natured. She needed to know how we were going to manage all the memories. She had a conversation with my psychologist and left very happy with what was transpiring.

Miss Sarcastic, my critical part, has a young helper now. She is known as Miss Playful. When she presented, she said she can show Miss Sarcastic how to have fun and enjoy the here and now. My psychologist has also renamed Miss Sarcastic – she is now "The Protector". A softer title to try to help her realise that she is needed and we are grateful for her never-ending role of keeping Jo safe. Once "The Protector" understands that she is no longer in danger, that the threat of abuse no longer exists, she will be able to relax.

This is a wonderful example of how a part can change through EMDR. It's also the reason why my psychologist prefers to assign titles rather than names to my parts.

There is a little 6-year-old called Jade who looks after Amelia, the 12-year-old. Because Amelia holds so many traumatic memories, Jade was her tower of strength and a safe place to land after a memory surfaced. However, Jade wanted to hand over her responsibility and play. She was shown the safe place that was created in my mind. Jade is now happily playing with other young parts in "The Safe Room". Amelia will undergo more EMDR as memories surface, helping her to reconnect with the now and leave her abusive past behind.

Many young children have presented over the years. Some non-verbal, one was sucking their thumb, and one was in a wheelchair. Some have asked my psychologist, "Can we hide? Will you hide with me? He cannot see us – he will hurt us." Another little one, named Eve, presented so traumatised that she sat on the lounge in the corner of the room. She would not make eye contact with my psychologist. Eve whispered, "Shush, be quiet, don't talk," followed by lots of crying. The fear that was in their childlike voices was heartbreaking.

A 10-year-old, who my psychologist has met before, is a go-between for other parts. She decided to have a name and chose Lilly. She explained she was speaking for a part who held memories of the abuse by my gynaecologist. I named this part Bonnie – she eventually came forward and was extremely upset. Lilly and my psychologist helped her to calm down by doing a little bit of EMDR. In that same session another part, called "The Bodyguard", presented. His role was to keep the memory away so that Bonnie wasn't too upset.

Amazing – the parts were born to keep me safe from certain memories. Other parts were born to help traumatised parts cope with their distressing memories. It definitely takes a village to raise a child.

A fourth part was present that day also. An adult around 30 years old, Bella, who was extremely upset. Bella was saying, "My head hurts, my head hurts, I feel sick, I am dizzy, I need to lie down." She laid down on the couch and closed her eyes. My psychologist encouraged me to do butterfly hugs as she tapped on my knees. The pain that Bella was experiencing finally subsided and she could sit up. More knee tapping was done to help calm her down. Once Bella was calm enough for my psychologist to talk to her, she asked a few questions. My psychologist doesn't have to know what the memory is, but questions along these lines are asked when she sets up a memory for processing:

- "What image represents the worst part of the memory?"
- "When you bring up the image, what words describe the negative belief you have about yourself now?"
- "When you bring up the image, what would you prefer to believe about yourself now?"

A few more questions are asked to gauge the intensity of the memory before processing. After processing, there are further questions to determine the extent to which the memory has subsided.

In this particular session, my psychologist asked, "What image represents the worst part of the memory?" Bella was unable to answer. She didn't want to go there.

"How do you feel about this memory?" the psychologist prompted.

"I feel dirty."

"What would you prefer to believe about yourself now?"

"I am innocent."

After the reprocessing was done, my psychologist asked Bella again, "What would you prefer to believe about yourself now?"

"I am in control."

This is a good example of how EMDR works and how, after the reprocessing, a positive phrase ("I am innocent") can become even stronger ("I am in control"). If the memory is not known, EMDR work can be done to hopefully deplete some of the emotion stuck around the traumatic event. Knowing the memory is the best scenario, if possible.

In this instance, it was a long and emotional session for me, but hopefully my psychologist has made life better for those traumatised parts. This in turn helps me cope with my everyday life.

When Bella left, another part presented who wanted to talk. Ten-year-old Lilly returned with a question: "Is it okay for parts to tell adult Jo about memories she doesn't know, because she is writing her book?"

My psychologist spoke to any part that was listening: "It is okay to tell adult Jo about the memories as they cannot be cleared completely if she doesn't know about them. But not too many at once. Allow time for a session of clearing between telling more memories. We don't want adult Jo to be remembering all these bad events and have to sit with them for too long before they can be cleared."

CHAPTER 21

Will you take me away?

While a child lies waiting frozen in time and consumed with fear
She silently whispers once again the question that she holds so dear
"Will you take me away to our happy place where
the sun is shining and I am safe?"
The brave part of her steps into the space
holding the horror she knows too well
When the monster has gone she will return, another
secret she and her part will not tell
She will not cry, she will have no fear, her
precious little body will feel no pain
She and her brave part are safe once more from
the monster, until it happens again...
Will you take me away?

—Jo Wilcox

Ninety per cent of my abuses happened inside houses, places that should have been my safe havens, full of love and support. Instead, my home became a place of fear, pain and mistrust. Ultimately, resulting in a small child's belief that this place with windows and doors is a place of long-suffering agony.

Not being able to relax and enjoy the companionship of my husband while in my home, because of the fear of being watched, has stifled my existence. I have lost hours, days, weeks and sometimes even months, trapped in a bubble of fear and shame.

Uncovering more evidence that may contribute to my hatred of being watched is helpful. My life is governed by this. Whenever I feel like someone is watching me, I will retreat from the situation and hide. *If I am seen, I will be hurt.*

During the many times my step-grandfather abused me, I was standing in front of him. An episode comes to mind where I was talking to my parts at home, trying to see if anyone could help me understand why I hate being watched. I started to see pictures and videos play in my mind. A very disturbing memory unfolded. The twins, Jack and Jill, whom I met back in 2000, presented. They were holding this memory. I was told that this memory and others like it were too traumatic for me to remember.

The twins were born to help me cope. Memories of my step-grandfather sitting in a chair, his erect penis in front of me, flooded my mind. The twins helped as much as they could to suppress the confused and fearful emotions I was feeling. In this particular memory, my step-grandfather grabbed my tiny hand, wrapped it around his penis, put his hand on top of mine and started to masturbate. I was trapped, unable to remove my hand, unable to escape. His excited eyes were watching my every move while my terrified eyes couldn't break the stare that connected the both of us in time.

This episode has been lessened a little by working with my psychologist, helping to overcome my debilitating shame of being watched. I mentioned to my psychologist that I was so worried I was making these things up.

"Remember you are not making this up," she said. "It is the way your brain has compartmentalised things that have happened, that is all. But there will be more because there are a lot of layers. But you can get there. You have more memories and also more communication now."

It breaks my heart that the person I most often retreat from is my husband. As I have said before, he never has and never would hurt me. I logically know this, but the all-encompassing fear I have – of him knowing what I am doing or that he may be watching me – has stopped me many times from doing things around the house or going out and enjoying myself. I do housework when he goes out. Running around like a mad person, getting as much done as possible.

I love being outside, mowing the lawn, weeding and making my yard look lovely. I feel free and unencumbered when I am outside. It doesn't bother me that my husband knows I am mowing. Although sometimes if I am extremely triggered, I won't even mow my lawn.

I have a large yard that is hilly with hard-to-reach places. One day in the middle of summer, when it was very hot and muggy, I was on the side of a hill, enjoying getting my hands dirty, trimming, weeding and being physical. I thought my husband was in the house, but I found out later that he was outside watching me. Not in a bad way – just making sure I was okay. I was engrossed in what I was doing and never saw him.

Later, he said, "I was watching you. I was worried it was too hot for you and you would get bitten by a snake." The horror I felt when I heard those words – "I was watching you" – was overwhelming. I didn't let on to my husband how triggering his words were. It wasn't his fault. I didn't mow the lawn for weeks after that. Instead, I sat in the trauma of childhood abuse and agonised, knowing I needed to be outside and moving around for my own peace of mind.

As I continued my sessions, three different young parts presented. They were all very worried about telling their secret. Ava said, "If I tell you the secret, he will hurt my sisters." Rosie said, "Jo used to talk to herself when she was little. If she did talk to herself, she would get flogged."

I understand now that I would have been talking to my parts, my imaginary friends.

It is very upsetting for me to hear that I may have been "flogged" for talking to myself. I do not remember talking to myself, so I do not remember if I may have been flogged. If one of my parts, maybe an angry part, presented while I was talking to my caregivers, they would take that as being disrespectful and I would have been punished – hence the flogging. Just a thought.

I do remember as a small child being told by my father, when I was in trouble, to pull my pants down, and lie face down on my bed so he could discipline me by hitting me across my bare bottom with his belt. Maybe this is what Rosie was referring to.

The last one was a new adult male. I called him “The Fixer”. His role was to stop me from being in freeze mode. He was a very strong physical part. When we lost the business because of our franchisor, I needed to earn some money. We were broke and I was trying to piece everything together again.

One day, I had a conversation with someone who needed a staff member. I started this job, which took me to many supermarkets and convenience stores. My job was to shelve all the bread after it had been delivered and to remove all the out-of-date bread.

I was so confident that I could do this work. Keeping in mind I was 69 years old, and 1.57 metres tall (five feet, two inches). I had to stack full bread crates as tall as I am. Maybe eight to fifteen kilograms in weight, depending on what type of bread or other product the vendor sold. I was working early mornings, which didn’t bother me at all. My confidence started to wane as more and more crates had to be moved from one location to another. But I persevered, the income being my driving force.

When “The Fixer” talked to my psychologist, he confessed that he signed me up for the bread job. Things started to fall into place because I was confused as to why I would do this job, as logically I would have known it would be a bit too much for me. I had to quit after a few weeks.

My psychologist talked to “The Fixer” and managed to convince him that there were more age-appropriate ways I could keep out of freeze mode. Another example of how amazing my parts are and the enormous impact they all have on my daily routine.

How do I cope with the never-ending switching between parts and their individual job descriptions? I have parts that want me to stay inside, safe and sound, together with parts who want me to move and not stay in freeze. Life is one big roller coaster ride, up one minute, down the next. Bracing for the loops and twists, and the inevitable emotional crash at the end of the ride.

My psychologist has told me it is good if I can talk to my parts on a regular basis. To reassure them they are no longer sitting in the trauma they protect me from. I have real difficulty with this. I even put a reminder in my phone, telling me to talk to my parts each day. But I find it difficult to do it on a regular basis. Because when I do, I could be confronted with another horrible memory.

Four parts presented at another session. Zoe, a very frightened five-year-old, just kept saying, "I don't want to. I don't want to do this anymore. I don't want you to hurt me anymore. I am scared." I found out that day that it was Zoe who caused me to dissociate while I was mowing my lawn. The fear she projected during the session was extremely upsetting for me. Some butterfly hugs were soothing and nurturing, helping her to calm down.

Millie, a nine-year-old, kept saying, "I have to be careful. I have to be careful." Some butterfly hugs were performed for her too. There was also a 40-year-old woman I named Patty. She was very caring, spoke softly and was very hurt that my mum didn't help to protect me from my step-grandfather. Patty was also very upset that Dad was horrible when he was drinking and I had to stay in my bedroom so I wouldn't get into trouble.

Another part, whom we called "Fierce Protector", also presented. She stopped me from talking to my other parts to help them realise they were safe. Her role was protecting me at any cost. Telling her she didn't have to do that anymore was hard for her to hear. "Fierce Protector" cried and cried, feeling the tremendous grief she had been holding for over 60 years. Not wanting to speak herself, she listened and spoke through Patty. "Fierce Protector" felt better when the session ended and wanted to talk again. Maybe next time she will be able to talk for herself.

How do I thread a needle between what my parts need to heal from their past traumas, and what I need to heal from my everyday existence?

Maybe you have realised by now that there is more than one part who helps with the same memory. A few are protectors. They all hold a certain aspect of the memory and therefore protect me in different ways, with the ultimate goal of keeping me safe. There are many young parts who are terrified because of the abuses they have endured. There are also many parts who band together to keep me closeted, making sure I don't venture out into the scary world. My EMDR work is helping these parts stand down and realise that the trauma has passed – that it is their time to relax and be proud of themselves for what they have done for me over the years.

There is another adult protector part who didn't want me to go out of the house. His name is John. He told my psychologist, "I am so used to keeping Jo safe I don't know how to change. I am upset she is telling all the secrets, because she will get hurt. She cannot write the book with all the secrets." My psychologist talked to John at length, explaining that we were no longer in trauma. John realised that it was okay for Jo to go out and have a life, as she is older and can look after herself. John was happy with that and will do all he can to help.

With John's help, Bessie, a young part, presented. My psychologist hadn't met her before. She was very upset and said, "We have to hide." This part grabbed three cushions and put them on top of herself. She covered herself up as best she could so no one could see her. She was petrified. My psychologist tried to console her, telling her she was safe and no longer in trauma. Bessie couldn't stop crying, bending her head down into the cushion so my psychologist couldn't see her.

"The man is watching me do things I didn't want to do and then he hurts me," Bessie said.

My psychologist tried to get her to look around the room and see that she was safe.

"Look at your hands – they are 69-year-old hands," my psychologist coaxed. "You have children now and grandchildren. Kylie, Guy, Hannah, Oscar, Archie and little Ivy."

My psychologist noticed that my left hand was caressing my right hand; 69-year-old Jo was comforting Bessie by lovingly stroking her hand. She started to cry when Oscar was mentioned.

Bessie said, "I feel sick."

My psychologist asked, "What do you need?"

"I am very tired and I want to go."

Before she left, my psychologist asked if Jo and John would help Bessie realise that Jo's husband is safe. He isn't Jo's step-grandfather. My psychologist asked, "Do you ever look at Jo's husband?"

"No, he wants to talk to me but I run away. I need to hide." Bessie left and so did John. Of course, if any of my parts are frightened of my husband, they avoid him, which means I avoid him. I run away.

I need to explain why I have all of these problems with my husband, and why my parts are terrified of him. As my husband has gotten older, remember he is 12 years older than me, he reminds my parts of my step-grandfather. They look nothing alike – it is just the old man look and certain mannerisms. Our early marriage was nothing like it is now. We were happy, did things together, and my parts had no fear of him.

My husband is so caring and tolerant of me. He does everything in his power to fit into the way I need to live to feel safe. I am getting better the more I see my psychologist, but some days I don't even want to see him, let alone have a conversation. The worst part is, he hasn't done anything wrong.

Unfortunately, my life experiences have taken a toll on our marriage. First step-grandfather's influence on my behaviour, dad's berating control, and then the constant financial woes since I married my husband. Years of stress and losses. Having to mend financial issues as best I could on my own. Maybe if I had been listened to, and good decisions were made, things may have been different.

In 2023 we separated after 29 years of marriage. We cannot afford to live separately as rents are too high and the age pension is our only income. It is not an ideal situation. My husband is constantly doing his best to accommodate my craziness. I try to get away and visit family so he has some down time. He can have the TV on super loud, cook what he wants and just chill.

Not being able to live on my own is incredibly triggering for me. As I have mentioned earlier, my husband had a session with my psychiatrist so he could hopefully understand the screwed-up way I need to live to feel safe. We have spoken together about what can help me to feel calm. He knows not to sneak up on me. Don't yell out to me. Don't cook meat while I am at home. Don't invite your friends or family to the house without me knowing. Don't make me feel like I am being watched. Don't touch me unexpectedly. He connects his TV through his hearing aids so I cannot hear it. Although it's best to follow these don'ts if we are to have any type of normal life, they fuel my self-loathing – like throwing too much kindling on an open fire.

Treating my husband like this distresses and saddens me. He is definitely not deserving of a life of constriction at his age.

This wonderful man took on my two kids. He loved, accepted and encouraged them. He helped with the early morning swimming training runs. And he was as proud as punch when Kylie and Guy did well at school and later on, in their careers.

When my grandkids come along he was their granddad, just not by blood. He cuddled, played and loved them unconditionally. He helped them build things for their school projects. Helped with the pickups from day care and then school. Missed Hannah terribly when she left for New South Wales. Was the go-to person for the grandboys when they were working on Ronda, the red hot Honda. Grandad had the answers to all their mechanical questions, sharing his many years of experience with them.

Along with me, he grieved, and is still grieving, the passing of our grandson Oscar.

A mind divided becomes the perpetrator of hurt. Ignoring the love that is hidden in plain sight. Leaving fear the manipulator.

My actions of avoidance as a child have accompanied me into my old age. Feeling the same emotions now that I felt growing up only exacerbates my financial ruin, another failed marriage, and my failure to change my performance in my old age. My father's negative appraisal of me is still haunting me. Still controlling me, still overshadowing me. My life is still not my own.

The hatred and abandonment I felt from my mother also weighs in on how my childhood wrote the screenplay for my adult years. It is not that easy to change what has already been written. It is not that easy to erase the adulterated memories of my childhood so that they do not impact negatively on what I could be as an adult. Each day I have something degrading to say to myself. My self-loathing never leaves me. It's a constant reminder of my parents' warped love. It is also a constant reminder of a life lost, and a brain that malfunctions on a regular basis because of how it was manipulated while it was still developing.

CHAPTER 22

Scars

Scars are not to be hidden.
They are to be acknowledged as life lived,
battles won and lost,
and the acceptance of our true imperfections.

—Jo Wilcox

As I have mentioned earlier in my book, we all have memories, good and bad. During a session, an adult part called "The Keeper" presented. I had just visited my sisters, and we were talking about good memories from our past. My sisters and their kids would often visit, and we would all venture to the beach to swim, play in the sand and enjoy each other's company. My nephew Andrew reminded me recently of the Christmas we had at my place. Lots of laughter and crazy play made for a beautiful day. I loved having all my nieces and nephews around; happy times. Unfortunately, I didn't remember a lot of what my sisters were talking about. "The Keeper" held on to good memories too and he had access to information from other parts.

My psychologist asked him, "Is there a reason why it would not be considered good to have access to good memories?"

"If Jo remembers good memories, then she would not want to work on the bad memories anymore and therefore not get well," he replied.

My psychologist proceeded to show him why having good memories would help. She used the Adaptive Information Processing (AIP) model. It explains how the brain processes memories and is the basis for EMDR therapy. The brain processes and links traumatic memories in a crude state, which leads to symptoms like PTSD, depression, anxiety or chronic pain. This model also recognises that both good and bad memories influence a person's current perceptions, behaviours and feelings. For example, eating a meal of liver, bacon and gravy. The bacon and gravy (good memories) make it more tolerable to eat the liver (bad memories). I don't like liver. How about you?

"The Keeper" was able to get information from other parts. They remembered that when Jo's kids were little, she used to take them for fish and chips by the water on the calm side of Bribie Island. "The

Keeper" said, "Only one memory today, as Jo felt it strongly and felt it in her heart." I did not remember this memory of me and my kids. This session blew my mind.

While I was with my sisters, they told me that I had saved a child's life in the ocean while we were on holidays on the Sunshine Coast. At the time, I was only a child myself but I was a good swimmer. I didn't remember this either, but I do now.

I cannot see how old we were at the time, but I can see myself holding the hand of this child, whom I didn't know, as we bobbed up and down, under and then on top of the waves. We were being dragged out to sea. I wouldn't let go of her hand. I tried to raise my hand so we could be seen from shore. We were eventually seen by the lifeguards and rescued. The lifeguard told me that if I hadn't kept holding this person's hand, she would have drowned, as she wasn't a good swimmer. My heart sings each time I remember this event. Something I can be very proud of. It is lovely to have good memories to brighten my day.

"The Keeper" has a big job keeping me on track. He is part of another DID phenomenon. That is, just because I am a female doesn't mean I will only have female parts. I don't see a picture in my head of my parts when they present. I feel their energy. Sad, angry, frightened or brave. My body feels big or small, even short or tall. When I am in session and the part speaks, that is another indicator of whether they are male or female, young or old.

The first time I realised a male part had presented, and I was also present, I was confused. I was having a wow moment. Trying to make myself stop feeling like a male was impossible. At that point in time, the male part was in control. Male parts are forceful, very determined and extremely protective. They all have their different ways of protecting me.

Tommy, who is a teenager, was angry as he helped me stand up to Dad by punching him in the stomach. Tommy didn't frighten me. On the other hand, "The Intimidator", who egged me on to stick a nail file in my arm more than once, frightened me terribly. It is a dreadful experience feeling so out of control that I cannot stop myself from self-harming. But that is how "The Intimidator" was trying to stop me from feeling like a useless piece of shit, a wimp.

It is hard not to judge my parts and how they have chosen to keep me safe. Feeling safe or feeling out of control, I wouldn't be alive today without them.

Believing in ourselves is so important to a happy life. The belief that I am not good enough has resonated with my soul for decades, allowing self-growth to be left locked behind impenetrable doors. The belief that I am worthless has left my energy bucket leaking hopelessly, leaving sludge where self-love could be. The belief that I am living outside of my own life proves that I am incapable of making decisions in my best interest. Believing that I am a capable, worthy woman, is not yet a known chapter in my book of life.

I have had many years on this earth, constantly trying to fit jigsaw pieces back in the right place. We all navigate around our own jigsaw board as best we can. A thousand puzzle pieces lay scattered, waiting for the moment we choose a piece and snuggly fit it next to its friend. I have walked away from my jigsaw board many times, allowing my self-hatred to convince me I am worthless. I do not deserve a puzzle piece friend to stand snuggly beside me, supporting me, encouraging me to step out and gather more puzzle pieces to make me strong.

Being constantly in a state of stress, we are out of balance, dysregulated, which is not good for the physical body nor the mind. Being regulated, in balance, is the ultimate goal of the human body. Stress is also a good thing. Back in the day, if our bodies weren't awakened by stress cues, we would have been eaten by our predators.

As babies, we were comforted by our parents. This comfort led to the knowledge that if we felt anxious or stressed, we would be soothed, held and loved. Our nervous systems were regulated and all was well in our world. In the case of children who are abused, either sexually or physically, or neglected, we don't receive the comfort we need to self-soothe and self-regulate. We receive a message that there isn't a warm embrace or calming words to save us. Instead, we are left to endure the abuse, unable to regulate our tiny bodily systems.

Dysregulation becomes our normal, causing our bodies to become unbalanced. Stress becomes our go-to emotion. No matter the circumstance, no matter where we are, no matter who is involved. An event that has pulled us back into our childhood abuses takes us back in time, allowing our body's systems to heighten all our senses to relive the abuse over and over again.

My crazy idiosyncrasies have come about from being constantly dysregulated. Like putting a pretty tea towel on the top of my bedside and lounge side tables so there is no noise when I put something down. Wearing ear plugs to bed because I cannot sleep if I can hear any noise. When I am extremely triggered, my ear plugs are accompanied by a pillow placed safely on top of my head. Using a sheet or blanket to cover me while watching TV if I feel vulnerable. Not wanting to do anything if I feel someone is watching me. Not going outside of my house when my fear barometer is off the charts. Shutting every window and door if I smell smoke, even if it is the middle of summer. Not wanting to dress up, or wear makeup, jewellery or perfume, and keeping a low profile so I am not noticed. Declining invitations when my hypervigilance is exposed, even though I know the inviter to be a safe person.

The main catalyst for DID is severe trauma during early childhood. Extreme repetitive sexual, emotional or physical abuse hinders the mental growth of the child. To escape the trauma, dissociation happens, leaving a lack of connection in a person's thoughts, actions, memories, feelings or sense of identity. Shutting down from the traumatic, violent or painful experience or situation is a life-preserving technique.

Almost 100% of people who develop a dissociative disorder have a history of recurring traumatic events, usually before the age of six. Neglect or emotional abuse, like parents who are frightening or unpredictable, can also cause a child to become dissociative. Living with DID, a complex posttraumatic development disorder, is a more common experience than we might think. Current evidence suggests that the prevalence of DID ranges between 1% to 3% of the general population. It affects women more than men. Traumas linked to DID include repeated physical, mental or sexual abuse, an accident, a natural disaster, military combat and being a victim of a crime.

There are many other mental health conditions that can accompany DID. Depression, mood swings, suicidal tendencies, sleep disorders, anxiety, panic attacks, alcohol and drug abuse, eating disorders, compulsions, rituals and psychotic-like symptoms. There is no cure for DID, although seeking professional help from an appropriate practitioner will hopefully lessen the burden.

I know I can do life on my own because I've proven it, but it is lovely to have family and friends wanting to come along for the ride. Even though telling my secret to my doctor almost 10 years ago was a good thing, I still struggle greatly with living, participating and enjoying life here on Earth. When Oscar passed, I wanted to go and be with him. My heart, which was filled with love, joy and hugs from my Oscar, was overflowing with grief.

Oscar and I had a beautiful relationship. I did see him in my dreams. We walked together, laughed together. We hugged, Oscar comforting me as I cried and cried. I miss him so much, his smiling face and eyes filled with love. Oscar's energy was radiant as it surrounded me in a rainbow-coloured embrace. I felt so blessed to have had this amazing reunion. The helplessness and hopelessness I feel here on Earth was lessened if only for a short while by the love I received from my heavenly grandson.

Dealing with Oscar's passing has left me grieving, unable at times to deal with my everyday life. I cry if a leaf falls off a tree, when his photo pops up on my mobile, when I see Clinkers on the supermarket shelves; Oscar loved Clinkers. The unpredictability of when I will burst into deep sobbing is uncomfortable. I cannot stop it, I cannot redirect it. I can only live with the grief that I feel from the deep love I shared with Oscar.

Grieving for her husband, Roy, my dear friend Lyn invited me to a "Reflection on Life" workshop run by Tying Up Loose Ends (TULE). An organisation that helps those who are dealing with the imminent death of a loved one, through to the immense grief that follows.

The morning of the workshop, I was so nervous. If I wasn't going with Lyn, I wouldn't have gone. The fear I was feeling had awakened my parts. They were working hard on my vulnerability, hoping they would win the battle, isolating me once more. As I entered the building, I could feel myself become so fearful of what, and who, I was going to encounter. I wanted to run away. Every fibre of my being was on high alert. My parts were engaged, ready to keep me safe, no matter what.

I met the facilitators – wonderful, caring ladies – as well as the other friendly participants. During the group meditation, whereby we stood in a circle in a beautiful garden, I began dissociating. My willingness to be anywhere else but there left me swaying backwards and forwards and around in circles as I tried my best to remain present and focused. I could feel my fear, and the sensation of being in mortal danger, flow through me. A sensation I have felt many times throughout my life. So I was not a novice to what was happening to me.

At the end of the meditation, we were asked to choose a card and to sit in a circle where we were told about our next task. We were to find a spot to write about the card we had chosen. We had one hour. When I read the card, something unlocked inside of me. At that moment, I didn't know what it was. Trying to hold myself together so the others did not know my anguish, I wandered around and found a beautiful spot to sit and reflect on the card I had chosen.

My card read: "Scar Stories – Tell about a scar, either one you can see or one that cannot be seen."

As I wrote my story, my emotions bought into my vulnerability with ease. Past hurts and events flooded my mind as my pen wrote words of pain. I finished my story and rejoined the others in our circle. The facilitator asked if anyone would like to share what they had written. One by one, beautiful, different and touching stories were shared.

Shaking like a leaf, my runaway emotions were filling every cell of my body. My hand shook as I fumbled trying to grab my journal. The next thing I knew, Miss Angry had presented and was swearing out loud at my dear friend, Lyn. As far as Miss Angry was concerned, it was all Lyn's fault that I was feeling so vulnerable, out of control and scared shitless. If Lyn hadn't invited me, I wouldn't be in harm's way. It only took a few seconds for Miss Angry's words to make me feel dreadful that I had spoken to my dear friend the way I did. I was mortified.

My head was swimming with so many thoughts. *I still have to read my story. I cannot do this. What does Lyn think of me? She must hate me. I cannot do this anymore. I hate having DID. I am so embarrassed. I want to disappear. I don't know these people. They must think I am a wacko. Why can't I stop shaking? I am going to be sick. I want to run away.*

I cried and shook as I apologised to Lyn in front of the others sitting in the circle. But those horrible words were already out there. I couldn't take them back. An apology will never fix what a part of me had ruined at that moment. The rest of the group could see that I was overwhelmed as I took a big leap of faith and read my story. My body released emotion after emotion. As my trembling hand turned each page, my teary eyes tried to make sense of my shaky handwriting. By the time I finished my story I was crying, trying unsuccessfully to hold back years and years of tears from the little girl denied her innocence to the grandmother losing her precious grandson.

My grief shook every part of my body while I sat in my chair, surrounded by strangers.

People I hadn't met until that day spoke calmly to me, reassuring me I would be okay, that they understood and were there to help me. Reminding me that it is a part of life to grieve. To feel all the emotions and to allow the release of those pent-up emotions. I was asked to take a number of deep breaths after which I eventually settled.

This is the story that I wrote in that beautiful, peaceful garden:

> "Is a physical scar worse than an emotional scar? It has been said that a physical scar will heal, leaving a mark and maybe a wound of sacrifice or trauma. An emotional scar can also be from sacrifice or trauma. But the traumatic emotion left from injury or harm is not seen, it is not heard and cannot be physically touched.
>
> Emotional scars are usually kept secret, buried beneath layers of other emotions in the too-hard basket. Our mind may venture from time to time to the abandoned scar, wondering if today will be the day we can assess and resolve the hurt, shame or guilt that our scar is wrapped in. Days, weeks, months or even years can go by without the need to visit this scar. Then one day a person or circumstance triggers this scar to become a fireball, too hot to handle without being burned. Our logical selves will jostle with our subconscious selves regarding the most emotionless way to deal with this out-of-control burn.
>
> Through years of living, our species has come to realise that a scar can be a thing of beauty, or a conquest over a beastly foe, giving the human a high standing in their community. A wound to wear like a badge of honour.
>
> But what if this scar is invisible? Does the scar become less than, because it is not displayed with honour? The repercussions of being scared emotionally are many and varied. If we are tainted by the many tentacles of this ghost-like scar, our world will be filled with doubts and fears. Traumatic abuse becomes our story,

while not coping with logical thought and reasoning becomes our overture.

A child is seen wearing a plaster cast adorned with squiggles, names and scribbled pictures. A happy ending to a broken leg. While the broken mind of another child is ignored. The once carefree, fun-loving child who has an invisible scar of abuse suffers in silence. Day in, day out, the abused child withdraws from play, focusing only on when the next atrocious liaison with her abuser will happen. Leaving her wondering how she will deal with the invisible aftermath of emotions that become her shield of shame and guilt."

Although that afternoon was extremely unsettling for me, I was grateful I was able to push through my vulnerability and overwhelming fear. I was grateful Lyn invited me and also so grateful that she understood and forgave me. Miss Angry had taken over my body because she felt I was in mortal danger. I was afraid, feeling vulnerable and not in control. In her eyes, I wasn't safe. If she didn't step in, I would get hurt. That day, I realised that I owned, and was reluctant to look at, a bucket full of guilt, shame and grief.

The threat my parts perceive is greater than my love of family or friends. If danger is imminent, the person my parts regard as the perpetrator will be the one in their firing line, either verbally or physically. It can only take seconds for me to dissociate and a part to present, portraying their displeasure of what is happening.

The parts that hold memories attached to smells and loud noises can present very quickly. A night with no sleep leaves me already strung out emotionally. Combine that with an extremely loud noise – like a truck backfiring, for example – and I am back in whatever trauma response surfaces first.

In one instance, my teenage self was exposed, remembering the loud, angry fights and the noisy drunken parties I lived through. My head filled with my father's belittling diatribes. My hope for a pleasant day was gone, replaced by hopelessness and the need to hide. I could feel the life drain out of me. I was cocooned in numbness.

All the candles are lit, and I am being sacrificed to my worthlessness shrine.

I sat for hours, watching TV that made no sense. The disconnection I felt from myself was overwhelming. I started to plan how I could self-harm. I worked it all out. Where I would leave my mark. How many times I would wound myself. Whether it would be letters, symbols, lines or just stab marks.

Knowing I have the power to harm myself, at any time, with any weapon, makes my heart race. I have control. I can pick and choose. It is my decision. Not my step-grandfather's, not my father's, not my gynaecologist's, or any other bloody male who mistreated me.

In the past, I have self-harmed due to uncontrollable rage, inconsolable sadness or unimaginable fear. Self-harming in response to a particular emotion is instant. No forethought. Just action, action, action. I am trying to release as much pent-up emotional energy as I can. Terrible pain is felt in every cell of my body.

In contrast, self-harming due to numbness is slow, precise, premeditated. The pain doesn't register. Watching blood ooze from my body invokes no response. Wanting to feel alive escapes me. Time stands still once again as I watch myself mutilate my body.

I understand there is no magical cure for my emotional and mental pain, although recognising when my parts are presenting is helpful. However, I feel DID will always be a misunderstood and confusing thorn in my side.

CHAPTER 23

Uncovering answers

There comes a time when I need control
To peel back the layers and save my soul
Many hurts I carry until my dying day
Through uneasy memories I will have my say
Frightened I will feel from time to time
But healing my heart and soul will be mine

—Jo Wilcox

Learning that I have been harbouring the silent emotion of loss, ever since I became a survivor of child sexual abuse, answers a lot of questions for me.

While these losses have left me struggling with sadness and how to express it, my lack of self-confidence has made writing this book incredibly difficult. I have dropped in and out of depressive episodes. I felt like I was in the spin cycle of a washing machine. Out of control, pinned against the side, having the life spun out of me. But it wasn't just life. They were memories, which I had trapped in a locked box and then thrown into the abyss long ago. I had every type of emotion explode out of my body. Many times, I walked away, wanting to curl up in a ball and hide, or punch the living shit out of something. I was stunned to discover how much I did remember in vivid colour as the tears rolled down my face.

Starting therapy later in life has left me with many years of trauma to heal from. It is a long and emotional road. The black hole that I tumble into when I am triggered is not easy to crawl out of.

I often ponder: *what comes first, the physical pain or the mental anguish?* My conclusion after years of both is that they go hand in hand; one feeds off the other. When I am living in my black hole, my ability to eat well and exercise is null and void. Happiness and the longing for human interaction are imprisoned in a padlocked room. Motivation is nowhere to be seen. There is only deafening stillness. Grey is my colour and hope eludes me.

The shame of wanting to see someone dead, and in the most horrific way possible, shows me how easy it could be for me to become the perpetrator. My step-grandfather is lucky he is already dead.

Learning to forgive myself for others' behaviours has been hard. Learning to forgive myself for my own behaviours has been even harder.

We can all be wise after the fact. Why didn't I tell someone? Why didn't I stand up for myself? Why am I such a coward? Why didn't I fight? A baby cries to get attention – feed me, change me, cuddle me. Her needs are met with love. A toddler cries but doesn't get the same response. She wonders what she has done wrong to have the people who once loved and cared for her abuse and mistreat her. A young child cries but she is told to stop whingeing. A teenager stands up and voices her opinion only to be knocked down, literally, for speaking out.

The blaming game has started. Whatever goes wrong in her world is her fault. The young adult starts to realise it is not worth the pain and humiliation to be heard. A pattern has been set, cemented fiercely into every cell of her body. She now becomes complacent, quiet, less than. She has learnt from an early age that her safety is her silence. To control her mental anguish, she must forgo herself and become a chameleon, fitting in seamlessly with every event and situation.

They say it is lonely at the top. It is also lonely at the bottom. When I am trapped in my black hole, there is only loneliness. The little bit of control I do have over my welfare is compromised. My parts have full control. Until they feel the threat has passed, I don't even consider trying to claw my way back to the top.

My days can be so different or unbearably the same. Days of pain can keep repeating, just like the sun rises each morning. A loop of depression and uncontrollable tears has me harnessed to memories I wish I didn't have. My anger can be triggered by the littlest thing. Accidentally dropping a spoon on the floor can awaken a self-hatred so terrifying that my wanting to become an angel becomes a mission and not just a passing whim. The immense feeling of being out of control, not being able to stop my temper from destroying everything around me, ignites my fawn response. I become frozen in time.

Scared but not being able to run, while anger runs around inside me, but I am not able to release it. I don't say a word. I isolate myself from family and friends. I stay as quiet as a mouse for as long as it takes. There is an overwhelming feeling that my life is not my own. A feeling that I will never have control of my life because my child sexual abuse is not easy to live with. My parts, who have, in their own way, kept me safe throughout my life, are also the ones who cause me so much pain.

Trying to overcome and forgive my screwed-up behaviours is hard when new memories come to light at almost every psychology session. Leading up to a session, I can become so distraught and terrified that I end up manifesting a physical illness so I don't have to go. This has happened many times over the years.

Unfortunately, these are the times that I need to go to my sessions. A part who is very upset, after being triggered by something in the present, needs to tell their story to be healed. They are reliving their trauma, and my fear and physical illness keep their secret from escaping. Constantly triggered, I am exhausted, buried under memories and traumas, trying to forget that which is unforgettable.

Waking one morning, I knew I was going to have a bad day. Having to be in my house triggered a cascade of emotions too forceful for me to handle. I knew I had to leave before I did something stupid. Fear was my trigger and anger was my weapon. I contacted my sister, Susie, who said I could visit. I hurriedly packed, jumped in the car and drove away.

There are a few parts who can produce an anger in me so strong that if I got in the WWE ring with Dwayne "The Rock" Johnson, he would be begging for his life.

This growing rage needed somewhere to go. I was a time bomb. I wanted to die, to crash, to leave this horrendous, soul-destroying planet. I felt my time was up. I couldn't take life anymore. My angry parts were ready to do their best to end my life. As I drove, I took stupid risks I would not normally do, yelling and screaming uncontrollably because my patience for other drivers was nil.

My road rage was epic. I was hoping a large, angry man would confront me. I wanted to fight to my death. No holds barred. Adrenaline coursed through me like hot lava, igniting every self-loathing cell in my body. My muddled mind was full of negative thoughts that were bumping into each other.

Am I always going to be like this? No matter what I do, I never get better. My parts rule my life. I have no peace. I am a complete waste of space. The more I drove through the Brisbane traffic, the angrier I got. *People are pathetic drivers. No blinkers. Slow drivers everywhere.* I drove up to a very busy two-lane roundabout. With two vehicles in front of me, a gap appeared between the traffic approaching. I screamed, "Move! There is a gap, you idiot. Move!"

My tolerance was nowhere to be seen. My compassion was having a holiday, and my common sense had flown out the window.

This was it – I was going to die. I drove straight onto the roundabout – I was not clear of the oncoming traffic. Horns beeped at me, tyres screeched, and smoke filled the air as drivers slammed their feet on their brakes in an effort to avoid a collision. I didn't care less. I wanted to die. I wanted to live on a cloud with Oscar.

Tears rolled down my trembling face as I realised. I was alive. I had dodged a bullet. Then the negative talk started. *You cannot do anything right. You are useless. A piece of shit.* Within seconds, my demeanour changed. I was scared, upset and bewildered.

A different part was my passenger now. Their voice invaded my mind. *What are you doing? You could have killed people – mums and dads, children, babies. You don't want that. You wouldn't hurt people deliberately.* As that realisation dawned on me, I was shaking. I was talking to myself out loud as snot ran out of my nose into my mouth.

"I can't do this anymore. I am never going to feel better. Why can't I be fixed? I have tried everything I could over the years. I am a good person. Why me? Why did he pick me? Why didn't Mum and Dad love me? Why didn't they save me? What is wrong with me?"

I was agitated, driving erratically through roundabouts, speeding along straight stretches of road, screaming, crying and wishing I hadn't been born.

I pulled up on the side of the road before I got to Susie's. I wiped my face, blew my nose and tried to make myself look like I hadn't been crying and playing dodgem cars with the unsuspecting traffic. Choosing carefully from my mask cupboard, I donned my mask of happiness, secured it tightly and drove into Susie's garage and parked. I was in one piece and I hadn't killed anyone, which I was so grateful for.

I got out of the car with a bounce to greet both Susie and my 2-year-old great-niece, Sophie, with a big smile and a wave. I had made it. Two-and-a-half hours of sheer torment had come to an end. Happiness and cuddles were waiting for me as I climbed the stairs. That night, the enormity of having DID, and what could have been a disastrous result, hit me like a wrecking ball. My parts could have killed innocent people. *Am I ever going to be at peace?* As I tried to go to sleep, I remembered a session with my psychologist where a part told her he had taken over the steering wheel and driven my car. How scary is that?

There have been so many times throughout my life that I have wanted to be dead. I wanted all of it to stop. The pain, the guilt, the shame. The emotions that cause me so much upheaval.

At my next psychology session, after I got home from Susie's, a part presented that thought she was already dead. This is what transpired.

Sitting on the lounge in my psychologist's room, I was feeling a lot of pressure in my head. I thought I was going to get a migraine. I kept staring at the floor, banging my palm against my forehead. I wouldn't look up. I wouldn't look at my psychologist. A part called Sadie had presented. I never looked up once while the part was present.

Sadie was mumbling, "My head hurts. I have pressure in my head. What is happening to me?"

My psychologist asked, "Why are you feeling pressure?"

Sadie replied, "I just want to die."

I was seeing a vision in my head of a teenager lying on the ground, dead. It was me. The terror I was feeling was unbearable. I thought my head was going to explode.

Sadie said, "I am dead."

My psychologist got me to do some tapping on my arms to help Sadie calm down.

She was asked, "Who did this?"

Her answer, "The boys."

I was experiencing a memory of a group of boys attacking me. I couldn't see the event, but the emotion attached to it was so traumatic I thought I had died.

My psychologist asked Sadie, "How old are you?"

Sadie replied, "I am 15."

Words buzzed around in my head. *Guilt. Shame. Grief. It was all my fault. I let this happen.*

My psychologist could see something was going on. "What is happening?"

I was shaking and sobbing uncontrollably as the part answered. "It is all my fault. I put myself in harm's way. It is all my fault. I just want to die. I want the pain to go away. I am so tired. I want to die."

My psychologist said to Sadie, "You don't want to die. You want the pain to stop. You want to stop hurting."

We did more tapping to help process the feeling of wanting to be dead.

After Sadie left, I asked my psychologist, "Was this the part that keeps telling me I should be dead?"

She replied, "Maybe, although there are probably other parts that also feel this way."

I do not have a conscious memory of this trauma. I walked away from another extremely upsetting session, wondering why I was going to therapy. More heartache and overwhelm to deal with.

Parts, parts everywhere! I have also realised that I am jealous of all the airtime my parts get. Crazy, right? I don't ever seem to get couch time with my psychologist to just talk about my week, my feelings, my everyday stuff. I am more aware of my parts now that I can feel when a part is presenting. So, I know when my session is going to be dominated by my parts. I know, I know – I am my parts, and they are me – but this is how I feel sometimes. Railroaded, left out, overlooked. I have spoken to my psychologist about this. Maybe I have a part who is making me feel this way? Wouldn't that be ironic?

Not so long ago, I was so upset with my parts that I went back to my sexual abuse counselling service. I thought it would help me to talk to them, one on one. I had a very informative conversation with the counsellor. In essence, it would be too confusing for my parts to have another form of counselling in addition to the EMDR with my psychologist. Well, that went down like a lead balloon for me. Again, it is all about my parts. After I had some time to digest what I was told, I agreed.

At the end of the day, I am also extremely thankful that I have my army of warriors who put themselves in harm's way so I didn't have to hold memories of absolute degradation, humiliation and pain. The network that these parts have is incredible.

At a recent psychology session, a young part presented. I will call her Debbie. My psychologist and I were talking about me not being able to go out into my own yard or go and see friends. I had been chained to my lounge chair for a few weeks. The thought of venturing outside sent waves of fear over me – from the top of my head to the tips of my toes. Having no idea why I felt the way I did was unbearable.

Debbie was crying to the point of hysteria. She started screaming. "It hurts – don't hurt me." My psychologist had to speak loudly to Debbie so she could hear over her screaming. She was so deep into the memory of my step-grandfather's abuse that nothing settled her. I was also present throughout this episode. I was a mess, emotionally and physically. My nose was running while the tears were never-ending. I was struggling to see, as my prescription glasses were all fogged up. Some time passed, with my psychologist talking calmly and reassuringly to Debbie. My psychologist told Debbie she was no longer in trauma. She was now an adult with children and grandchildren.

Once Debbie had settled down, my psychologist offered me a tissue to blow my nose and asked if I would take my glasses off, so I could wipe them. I have experienced strange happenings over the many psychology sessions I have attended, and this one was no exception.

The second I removed my glasses, Debbie became hysterical again, more so than before. My arms were flailing around while my legs were shaking and jumping. I had absolutely no control over what was happening to my body. My psychologist had her work cut out for her, trying to hold Debbie's attention through screams of petrified vulnerability.

Thankfully, within minutes my psychologist asked me to put my glasses back on. Instantly, I could feel my body release the stifling fear that had hijacked me. Debbie, who had protected me from this memory for years, cried tears of release.

Eventually, a calmness filled the room as my psychologist waved her magic wand of healing.

At the end of my session, I asked my psychologist why there was such a violent reaction to me taking my glasses off.

Her response was, "Your glasses are a symbol of being old. Taking them off, Debbie was immediately back in the terrifying memory."

As I have mentioned throughout my book, I have had many suicide attempts and self-harm episodes. It is difficult to manage my stress, anxiety and depression while parts of me are dealing with triggers that occur in my everyday life. I have had to learn self-soothing and grounding techniques to keep me in a place of relative balance.

Giving and receiving hugs is also a great way to calm your nervous system. When I am on my own and I need to settle down, I place my hand over my heart. Doing this affects the same part of your brain that a hug does. Breathing slowly, while holding your hand on your heart for a few minutes, helps to soothe your anxiety.

Another good exercise is to breathe slowly while looking around at your surroundings. This involves using your five senses: sight, sound, smell, taste and touch.

What can you see? Furniture, photos on your wall, your loving pet, trees, flowers.

What can you hear? Music on your radio, traffic going past, birds chirping.

What do you smell? Coffee or tea you made earlier, a candle, yummy food.

What can you taste? Leftover tastes from food or drink, or even your own saliva.

What can you touch? The fabric of the chair you are sitting on, your clothes, your hair blowing in the breeze as you walk along.

This exercise helps you to ground your energy.

When we are grounded, we feel calmer.

CHAPTER 24

Recovery

May your eyes dance happily along your path of
self-discovery
May your nose smell fragrant aromas from your
life's garden
May your ears hear joyous conversations from your
inner wisdom
May your mouth speak with words full of
mindful awareness
May you always feel peace and harmony throughout
your journey
May your heart be open to receive your own
self-compassion
May your mind allow you to unlock your inner child,
so you may live and play with carefree abandon
You are exceptional

—Jo Wilcox

Many years ago, my husband and I took our granddaughter, Hannah, on a holiday when she was around three or four years old. It was a bright, sunny day, full of laughter and play. We had returned to our unit after having a swim, ready for some lunch.

"Come on, Hannah. Let's sit on the balcony and watch the world go by," Granddad beckoned to her.

He lifted her up onto the chair and handed her a plate of yummy sandwiches. I could see that Hannah had a puzzled look on her face. With the innocence and wonderment of a happy child, Hannah asked, "Where's the world, Granddad?"

"It is everywhere that you can see, sweetheart. The people walking around, the blue sky, the ocean – everything. Do you understand?"

With a mouth full of food, Hannah managed a stifled, "Yep."

The innocence of a child filled my heart with joy. The three of us sat silently together, eating our lunch, content in watching the world go by.

Being groomed before I even had conscious memories meant I grew up not knowing who I truly was. My life has always been what others wanted it to be. The small, pretty thing who played her part, albeit unknowingly.

Experiencing trauma throughout my life has left me with a long list of mental, emotional and physical challenges, explored throughout this book. They have captured me like the cookie thief who has their hand stuck in the cookie jar. Not until the cookie thief lets go of the cookies will the jar relinquish its hold and allow them to escape.

Letting go of the proverbial cookies in the cookie jar is the ultimate goal for a trauma survivor, allowing freedom from the confines of a trauma-fuelled life.

My situation is doubly difficult to overcome as I have the added trauma response of dissociation.

Constantly living in the shadow of known and unknown memories, which haunt my nights and smother my days, leaves me in a state of procrastination. My inner fight to regain some sort of forward momentum becomes harder than jogging up Mount Kosciuszko, Australia's tallest mountain. I watch myself sit, scared and alone, wanting to be present in my life. Wanting to be productive. Wanting to be healthy and wishing to be happy.

Through my counselling, I have learned that procrastination can be a trauma response. My understanding is that in order to protect itself, my childhood brain avoided stressful situations at all costs. Leaving my internal motivational drive irrelevant.

The delaying, postponing or even cancelling of activities is governed by my ever-present state of procrastination. Medical appointments, family gatherings and get-togethers with friends become second fiddle to my need to stay safe and out of harm's way. Of course, now that I am an adult, I am no longer in danger. My abusers are dead. So, why am I still neck deep in a vat of fear? Because my parts are actively trying to keep me safe.

Staying out of sight, quiet, inconsequential and irrelevant, is how my parts keep me alive. My logical mind, my rationale, has no say whatsoever in this behaviour. I am just a foot soldier, taking orders from those in command – my parts. My depression, loss of motivation and, on some occasions, manifested physical ailments are my world. Happiness is a swear word. Productivity is a no-show. Desperation to see my family and friends eats away at me. My self-hatred is all-consuming. The lies I tell, to justify my absence from appointments and events, compound the guilt and shame as I sit in my lounge room, while my parts have hogtied me to my abusive past.

Yet, when I do venture outside and try to engage with my world, my burdens become smaller. I find my smile. I remember how wonderful it is to have a conversation, to open my heart without trepidation. Like many things, joyous repetition is available to us once we acknowledge our present habits of mistrust, self-loathing and worthlessness. Bit by bit, day by day, we can replace old habits with new, positive, thought-provoking ones, leading us to become willing participants in our world.

Keeping active is an easy way to help your sanity. Walking, swimming, cycling – anything that gets you out of your lounge chair. I have ventured back to the botanical gardens. Constantly working on my triggers and fears with my psychologist has helped me to understand that I am safe.

My love of nature soothes me as I walk briskly along the winding tracks, through the trees, over the small streams, and up and down the many hills. I love looking at the different sculptures and plants and reading about their history. Pleasure outguns my fear by helping me enjoy my world.

Maybe "The Fixer", who wants to keep me out of freeze, has a hand in my decision also. But this time, it is an exercise I can do and that I love. He also listened and learned from my psychologist.

Pushing myself to smile and say hello to complete strangers is becoming easier each day. Eye contact and a little smile cost me nothing to share. You never know. One day, my acknowledging another human being may stop that person from going home to binge eat uncontrollably. They may not keep walking to the liquor store to buy huge amounts of alcohol to drown their sorrows. Their thoughts of suicide may fade away for another hour, day, week or even a year – just because a connection was made.

I am lucky I have reached old age. There have been many times I have wished to leave this world. There have been many times I was so grateful to be alive. I understand my pitfalls and do not wish my plight of mental health challenges upon anyone. When I can, I help my fellow human beings. On many occasions, I have seen a person in a predicament and offered to help. It only takes a moment to lend a hand.

I want so desperately to overcome my traumas, to live my life, to pull back the pieces of me that are floating aimlessly in the ether. Ultimately resembling a patchwork quilt, full of beautiful colours, with my many different parts lovingly sewn back together, completing a story that began fractured but ended with my body feeling like a loving home, safe and full of purpose.

I often wonder how I have got this far in my life. I wish I knew. I have stumbled many times, becoming overwhelmed by whatever situation or event showed up for me to deal with. The same old question emerges: *if I told my story to a professional years ago, would I be as broken as I am now?*

I asked my psychologist and this was her answer:

"Most of Jo's parts are below 30 and she had a lot happen in these first 30 years. Hence, it would still have been long-term therapy. There are certainly benefits starting earlier. However, the fact that Jo has had longstanding, trusting and loving relationships for so many decades means that parts are able to trust Jo – that she knows how to keep them safe now, and that she is loved in a healthy way, and that she has healthy attachments. This makes the reprocessing easier because there is a lot of evidence that she is safe and has been safe and in loving relationships for a long time. So there is a lot more adaptive information than there may have been earlier. This is helpful in the work we do."

My sister, Lisa, lives on a farm. During a visit, I had the opportunity to observe wildlife in their natural habitats. Sitting in the paddock early in the morning, it was so quiet. Only the birds and animals were making noise. I watched a little joey kangaroo. He looked at me to make sure he knew where I was. Satisfied he was safe, he hopped around, eating grass and watching out for anything that might hurt him.

If my life had been like the little joey kangaroo's, my heart would be full of joyful wonder, my mind full of peaceful thoughts.

A beautiful king parrot flew down from the tree and wanted some food, sunflower seeds probably. I didn't have any. I just had a banana. *Oh well – they eat fruit and seeds.* I threw him a bit of my banana. He ate it and hopped over to me and up onto my chair. He had some more banana and looked in my teacup. Still very curious, he jumped up on my garden hat. Not concerned at all, he enjoyed the serene surroundings from his perch.

I was sure he had been a pet at some stage, or he had been a rescue, because he was so friendly, and he only had one claw. This beautiful bird had been looked after and nurtured. He was not afraid. It is a shame some humans don't look after their own as well as we look after the animal kingdom.

I sat in this beautiful space, taking in the majesty of the early morning sun peeking through the trees, providing light, warmth and hope for the new day.

The little joey was sitting at the gate. He had finished eating grass. I wondered if he was thinking: *do I jump over the gate or go through the fence? Where is my mum*? He looked at me, not sure what to do. He decided to go through the fence. So, he worked out what he needed to do to get to the other side of his barrier. This is what I have to do. I have to work out what I need to do to get on the other side of my trauma barrier.

Life is not easy for any of us. Unburdening ourselves of secrets and life's many struggles does help. Before I started therapy, there was just a very large, high brick wall stopping me from growing past my traumas. Fear, immobilising fear, was the culprit.

Not helping my young mind grow up, in the best way possible, smothered what should have been my joyous exploration of life. Instead, my young mind developed haphazardly. I didn't get any professional play therapy, cognitive behavioural therapy (CBT), or progressive psychotherapy treatments like EMDR. So, my memory train just kept adding carriages full of soul-destroying situations that my parts helped me to forget, weighing me down, not allowing me to function in the typical way at any age throughout my life.

My counsellors have told me that because of the abuse I suffered as a small child, my cognitive function, the ability to form satisfying relationships and my self-worth have all been impaired. My hippocampus, which is responsible for memory and learning, may not function properly. My early sexual abuse may have also affected the development of my prefrontal cortex. It is fascinating how the human body functions. But it is also terrifying how early traumas can impair or even halt the natural progression of our mind's growth.

Young or old we crave love but, sometimes, are too fearful to seek it out. As social beings, staying closeted with no human interaction kills our soul. When we venture outside of our comfort zone, many things may worry us, but many things may also fascinate us. We can all read book after book, but, until the response to trauma affects us personally, it is hard to truly understand.

I cannot fight an enemy I don't understand.

It is 2025. I am officially a member of the old farts club. My seventieth birthday was celebrated at home with Kylie, Guy and Sarah. We all had a beautiful time, enjoying each other's company and conversation. Hannah, Marc and Ivy wished me a happy birthday from afar. I received many birthday greetings from family and friends. No big bash for me – an intimate gathering full of love was all I needed. Archie arrived later in the day and slept over, which was an added bonus. Having him close is healing for me. We enjoyed a wonderful, peaceful and happy evening together. The next morning, he left to spend the day with his loving mum before heading back to Brisbane.

I will be working on many things in my life in this coming year and beyond. Things that have held me back from being the person I know I can be. They are many and varied. I may not succeed at resolving them all. To stay focused on the positive and be kind to myself will be a good start.

I would love to start the day with a smile, wanting to be present and grateful to be alive. For my husband and me, even though we are separated, to be friends and have cuppas and chats together, instead of always giving him a wide berth, fearful of being touched. I would love to smell coffee, meat cooking, smoke and fumes without reacting negatively. To venture outside spontaneously without fear of being hurt by the unknown. Feeling safe, tranquil and happy in my own home, to set goals and realise them with courage, creativity and passion. Trusting the process is a big one for me, but there is no reason why I cannot eventually trust myself and others.

My ultimate goal: to no longer live just in my head, but to live in my heart as well.

One thing that I do not have to worry about anymore is my drinking. I have been sober for almost 10 years.

They say time heals all wounds. The only thing time does is show us how little of it we have. Time plays with our fragility. Our healing is relative to the time we spend mending ourselves. That is why it is so important to not waste time, to harness it, to have it work for us and not against us. My time so far, here on Earth, has been wasted by fear. I have been tortured by watching time slip by me because my abuse has kept me in lockdown. Hours, days, even weeks have slithered past without even a hello. Time is a precious commodity, something we truly do not get back. Each minute of time can be so different. Filled with happiness, sadness, fear, vulnerability, anger, hatred, love or laughter. How we chose to spend our time is so important.

We all need love. Self-love especially, and to appreciate who we are. Without self-love, we will not mend. When we show compassion to ourselves and the life we have endured, then our healing will begin.

Remember, recovery is a team sport.

Be willing to be open-minded, even if you don't believe everything a professional tells you at first. Turn up, sit up and listen. Push through your debilitating fear. Your healing will take time, but it is you who does the healing, who closes that gaping wound, with the help of Father Time, family, friends and your professional team.

I started my healing late but I still have time on my side. Through my perseverance and a desire to be healed, my mindset will change, allowing me to feel worthy of abundance and prosperity. A passion for life will envelop me. Self-confidence will be my smile, happiness will be my barometer, and peace will fill my soul. My mind will follow my heart and be a vessel of positive, productive and meaningful thoughts.

I wish that for you, too. I wish for you to know that it's never too late to speak up. If you are old enough to tell your secret, do it. Take a deep breath and phone a trauma helpline. Find a trusted relative, friend, co-worker, priest, teacher, policeman – someone who will help you get the support you deserve. Use your precious time to heal and experience life in all its wonder.

It's time to break the silence.

Transformation

Life's Challenge

Change

Life's Constant

Acceptance

Life's Story

—Jo Wilcox

Acknowledgements

I would like to acknowledge the amazing people who over the years have touched my life.

My children, as well as my earthly and heavenly grandchildren. My husband. My sisters and their families. My extended family and families-in-law, ex and present. My aunties, uncles and cousins. My dear friends, lifelong and new. My Mum and Dad who did the best they could.

My professional medical team, my natural therapies team and my trauma counselling team. Work and volunteering colleagues, and amazing ladies I have met at therapy sessions.

Without each and every one of you, I wouldn't be here today. Many times, I received face-to-face encouragement, phone calls, text messages or emails, supporting me with love at crucial times in my life. Bringing me back from a life-ending precipice. Allowing me to regather and fight another day.

The love, respect, encouragement and non-judgement I have received has helped me to realise my dream to write my book.

Last but not least, my new friend and mentor, Roxanne McCarty-O'Kane. Her generosity, encouragement and unwavering professionalism has kept me moving forward when I found myself floundering. More than once, emotional upheaval stopped me in my tracks as I had to relive my traumas. Her kind words of support and her caring attitude allowed me to dig deep into my innermost self to tell my deepest secrets.

All of you have never questioned the authenticity of my life's story. Your unwavering belief in me as a person and as a writer has meant the world to me.

You have all seen me and believed me beyond expectation. Thank you from the bottom of my heart.

I would also like to acknowledge my many and varied parts. My army of warriors who for many years did their best to keep my safe. They endured horrendous and debilitating events, putting themselves in harm's way to shield my fragile being.

For the next chapter of my life, my wish is for my parts to realise it is now their time to relax, step back and enjoy the freedom of no longer being in trauma. My parts and I will go forward together, knowing we are now safe.

To the trauma survivor,

May you be forever hugged by love

Filled to overflowing with self-worth

Calmed by peace and self-awareness

Tickled by happiness and laughter

Accepted by self and others with open arms

Believed by all without exception

You are deserving, the wonder, who is you.

—Jo Wilcox

'Our brains are wired for connection,
but trauma rewires them for protection.
That is why healthy relationships are
difficult for wounded people.'

—Ryan North, Canadian Writer

Support resources

Australia

**** If you are in immediate danger, call 000 ****

- 1800 RESPECT – support if you, or someone you know, is experiencing sexual assault or domestic and family violence: 1800 737 732
- Beyond Blue – support for anxiety and depression: 1300 224 636, beyondblue.org.au
- Kids Helpline – for young people aged from five to 25: 1800 551 800
- Lifeline Australia – crisis support and suicide prevention: 13 11 14, lifeline.org.au
- Bravehearts – counselling and support for survivors of child sexual abuse: 1800 272 831
- Child Wise – counselling provider: 1800 991 099
- MensLine Australia: 1300 789 978
- PACT – for legal support: pact.org.au/
- Parentline: 1300 30 1300
- Queensland Sexual Assault Network: qsan.org.au/services/
- Suicide Call Back Service – free 24/7 telephone counselling support if you are at risk of or affected by suicide: 1300 659 467
- Victims of Crime Australia: victimsofcrimeaustralia.com.au/
- Tying Up Loose Ends (TULE) – supporting those who have experienced death, dying and grieving: tyinguplooseends.com.au
- White Eagle Lodge – a place of spiritual refreshment, a gentle home of the spirit: whiteeaglelodge.org.au/

New Zealand

**** If you are in immediate danger, call 111 ****

- 1737 – Free helpline, whereby you can call or text 1737 any time for support from a trained counsellor
- Lifeline: 0800 543 354 (0800 LIFELINE) or free text 4357 (HELP)
- Youthline: 0800 376 633, free text 234, email talk@youthline.co.nz or chat online at youthline.co.nz
- Samaritans: 0800 726 666
- Suicide Crisis Helpline: 0508 828 865 (0508 TAUTOKO).

United Kingdom

**** If you are in immediate danger, call 999 ****

- Find a Helpline – seek localised and specialised support: findahelpline.com/countries/gb/topics/sexual-abuse
- Mind – mental health support: 0300 102 1234
- National Association for People Abused in Childhood: 0808 801 0331, email: support@napac.org.uk
- National Suicide Prevention Helpline UK: 0800 587 0800
- Samaritans: 116 123
- SANEline: 0300 304 7000
- Sexual assault referral centres: nhs.uk/service-search/sexual-health-services/find-a-rape-and-sexual-assault-referral-centre
- Victim Support – operates a free and confidential 24/7 support line and live chat service, offering specialist support to anyone who has been a victim or witness of crime: 0808 168 9111, victimsupport.org.uk/live-chat, victimsupport.org.uk

United States of America

**** If you are in immediate danger, call 911 ****

- 988 Lifeline: Access call, text or chat at 988lifeline.org/get-help/
- Crisis Text Line: Text "HOME" or "HOLA" to 741741
- RAINN (Rape, Abuse & Incest National Network) – national sexual assault telephone hotline: 800 656 HOPE (4673)
- Victim Connect Resource Centre: Phone or text 1 855 4VICTIM (1 855 484 2846) or chat online at www.victimconnect.org

www.ingramcontent.com/pod-product-compliance
Ingram Content Group UK Ltd.
Pitfield, Milton Keynes, MK11 3LW, UK
UKHW020127290926
15471UKWH00003B/325